SHOOTING WOOD-PIGEON

SHOOTING
WOOD-PIGEON

By

A. E. B. JOHNSON

Drawings by Bert Smith

LONDON : HERBERT JENKINS

First published by
Herbert Jenkins Ltd.
3 Duke of York Street,
London S.W.1
1961

MADE AND PRINTED IN GREAT BRITAIN BY
WILLIAM CLOWES AND SONS, LIMITED, LONDON AND BECCLES

CONTENTS

LIST OF PHOTOGRAPHS

LIST OF DRAWINGS

INTRODUCTION

THE past few years have seen a steady increase in the popularity of pigeon shooting, brought about in no small way by the exit (temporarily?) from our sport of the rabbit —due to myxomatosis. Indeed, in some areas, the pigeon is practically the only quarry, apart from the odd Game bird, remaining for the sportsman to shoot. In this book I have endeavoured to cater mainly for the beginner, but I feel sure that the experienced amateur and possibly the few remaining professionals may glean still further knowledge from my experiences. The saying goes that, "one is never too old to learn".

There are several recognised methods of shooting wood-pigeons, and I have tried to cover these in as much detail as possible—with diagrams where required. It should, therefore, be possible for the reader to gain the fundamentals for ultimate practical success. Although the title mentions only wood-pigeons, it will be found that I have included the stock-dove (or "blue rock") under this heading. This smaller relative of the "woodie" offers very good sport, but does not tend to be quite so destructive to the farmer's crops. The rock-dove is excluded from this work, as, in The Protection of Birds Act, 1954, it became protected in England, Wales and Northern Ireland (although shooting is still legal in Scotland). My experience of pigeon shooting has been mainly confined, of course, to my home county of Essex. Here, a field of 40 acres is the exception rather than the rule. As in most sports, however, the sportsman must be prepared to adapt himself to the conditions prevailing in his own locality. I have devoted the earlier chapters of this book to the food and characteristics of pigeons, for really the first essential of pigeon shooting is to know where and when to go after one's quarry. One must, in fact, almost be able to think like a pigeon (and sometimes, literally, "coo" like one). The remaining chapters deal with the actual methods of shooting (e.g. over decoys, flight-shooting, shooting in woodlands, etc.).

No amount of reading can make up for practical experience in the field, but it can help the keen beginner along the road towards success. The details I have written in this book are almost entirely the outcome of my own experiences, and any method that is recommended to the reader has been fully proved in practice.

I feel that I cannot end this introduction without expressing my thanks to Mr. Bernard Downing, who provided the excellent photographs for this work, and also to Messrs. David Topley, Gilbert Lumsdaine, Jack Davey and Noel M. Sedgwick for their valuable assistance during the preparation of the text.

A. E. B. J.

PART 1

THE WOOD-PIGEON AND STOCK-DOVE

THE wood-pigeon or ring-dove is one of our commonest birds throughout the year in most parts of the British Isles. It is easily recognisable at close quarters with its pinkish breast, greyish-blue plumage and, of course, white neck "ring". The tail is black, with white undercoverts, whilst the feet and legs are pink. In the field, at a distance, the wood-pigeon appears to be a grey bird, with the white patches or "ring" on its neck much in predominance, especially during the breeding season (i.e. March to September). During the autumn and winter the "ring" is not so evident, and in young birds it does not appear until full plumage is attained.

In flight, the pigeon is amongst the fastest of birds in these islands. Normally, on a calm day, they seem to fly in a leisurely manner, but their speed can often be deceptive. The flight is usually high, direct and purposeful, with a certain amount of weaving. Once a pigeon is frightened by something, however, it proceeds to take violent evasive action. It will usually veer away at an angle, swerving from side to side into the bargain. If some trees are nearby, it will very quickly put one or more of these between itself and danger. Needless to say, a bird flying in this manner makes an extremely difficult target.

In a strong wind or gale there is a certain amount of rising and falling in the flight of pigeons beating upwind —as with other species of birds. Quite often, when suddenly confronted by a human, a pigeon will curl away with the wind until well out of range, and then proceed to fly upwind—well wide of its former course. One definite characteristic of wood-pigeons, but not always resorted to, is a kind of "whiffling" action when a flock is coming into land with, or flying over, a feeding flock. The birds seem to tumble and roll in the air, usually sweeping low over the ground. It always seems to be a symbol of greeting or perhaps pleasure. Rooks will also perform similar aerobatics, but I have never known stock-doves to behave in this manner.

The stock-dove or "blue rock", as we call it in my district, is a smaller bird than the wood-pigeon. It is neater in appearance and has no white "ring" on its neck. The plumage is blue-grey in colour whilst the double black bars on its wings are very noticeable as it flies low over the ground. The breast and underparts are a pale blue and it has a black tail and pink feet. The neck is tinged with green and purple, whilst the eyes are large, bright and altogether fitting for a truly sporting little bird.

In flight, the blue rock is very fast, direct, and minus the weaving of a wood-pigeon. Once danger is encountered, however, it behaves very wildly. Quite often, if flying at a moderate height, it will turn sharply at right-angles, flying at an angle of forty-five degrees towards (or away from) the ground until well out of danger. When a shot is fired at a small flock in flight, the birds fairly "explode" in all directions, making extremely difficult targets. This pigeon has keener eyesight than the wood-pigeon, and even the slightest movement of the waiting shooter is detected. This statement must not be taken as implying that the "woodies'" eyesight is suspect. How very wrong. Only rooks, carrion crows, magpies and jays have any quicker sight for detecting danger.

Whilst the wood-pigeon will normally land in a tree, if one is nearby, before going into feed on a field, the blue rock is more prone to landing direct, after a few circles to ensure that all is safe.

Blue rocks are extremely suspicious birds and often land far out in a field—rarely close to a hedge. They are very agile walkers, and it is surprising how quickly they move about when feeding. Being always on the alert, they will rise smartly if disturbed, and, when the danger is close at hand, will dart off very swiftly in a most erratic manner.

Pigeons have excellent hearing, and the snap of a dry twig or rustle of undergrowth is fully sufficient to set a roosting or feeding flock on the alert—and usually in flight. How many times have I managed to crawl almost within shooting range of a feeding flock, only to hear a clatter of wings as they have departed for healthier grounds. The smallest noise appears to register with a pigeon when even the human ear would hear nothing unusual—or at least that's how it seems.

The breeding season of the wood-pigeon is very pro-longed—to put it mildly. I rather believe that eggs have been found in every month of the year in this country. With odd exceptions, however, the nesting period is between late March and September, with the peak period being July to September. Nests have been found in all manner of places, but usually a tall hedge, tree, or ever-green shrub is preferred, and the materials used in construction are normally twigs and roots. The finished article looks a very flimsy affair, with practically a flat surface, and on this "platform" the hen bird lays her two longish white eggs. Quite often if the nest is near the ground, one can see the eggs showing through the bottom of the twigs. Considering that only two eggs are laid, and the awkward construction of the nest, it is difficult to realise that the wood-pigeon is actually on the increase in some parts of the country. Of course, the pigeon does have three broods in the breeding season—and possibly more eggs are laid if a mishap occurs—so that perhaps in this way a flourishing population is maintained.

On being disturbed from its nest, a pigeon will usually flap low over the ground—in a wounded fashion—trying to draw the human away from the nest. During incubation, which takes seventeen days, the parent birds usually take turns at sitting on the eggs, and when the young arrive, both birds are engaged in feeding duties. The youngsters are fed by regurgitation, and are often called "squeakers" or "squabs" whilst they are fledglings. When they are hatched, they are covered in fine yellowy hair which in due course gives way to feathers. Once fully fledged—about a month after hatching—the young pigeons soon learn how to fly, and flap into nearby trees where the parent birds bring their food supply. After a few days at this stage the youngsters gradually begin to follow their parents on trips to the feeding grounds and eventually learn to feed and take care of themselves. During their early flying days young pigeons fall easy prey to the sparrow hawk and other birds of prey, but soon they become just as wary as their parents.

The breeding habits of the stock-dove are in the main very similar to their larger relation—with the exception of the nesting site. As implied by its name, the stock-dove normally chooses a nesting site in the hollow of a tree, although they will nest in holes in quarries, cliffs, etc. (as does the rock dove), and I have known them to use the disused nest of a magpie. One rather peculiar site that I came across last spring was a nest in one of the small gaps left between the bales in a large heap of straw bales. The eggs of the stock-dove are laid a little earlier in the year than most wood-pigeons, and consequently young birds are in evidence earlier. In Essex, this pigeon seems to have a distinct liking for the holes in old willow trees, and often there are two or three nests close together, in neighbouring

The quarry—the adult wood-pigeon. It has a white patch on its neck
and is built sturdily.

The Stock-dove. It has a bright eye, black wing-bars and glossy-
green neck feathers.

trees. The sitting birds are very alert and depart from the nest at the slightest noise in the vicinity. The birds dart out of the nesting holes flying low over the ground, and only return when danger has passed.

It is a sure sign that spring is really with us when the stock-dove can be heard cooing, in the misty dawn, from the willows that stand beside some quiet meandering stream. The peaceful song seems to incorporate all the freshness of the dewy water meadows and the smoothness of the water as it glides over the shingle beds into a calm deep pool. William Wordsworth, a great lover of nature, describes this bird and its song in his poem *Resolution and Independence* when he says, "over his own sweet voice the stock-dove broods". These brief words express the very essence of this neat little bird.

Courtship is a characteristic of all species of birds, and both the wood-pigeon and stock-dove indulge in "courting" flights. It is very pleasant on a bright summer's day to watch a wood-pigeon behaving in this manner. An outburst of cooing usually heralds one of these displays, and the actual flight consists of a series of graceful climbs and glides with strong wing claps just before the peak of each climb is reached. The bird generally flies in a circle—returning to its original perch. Quite often, however, the flight terminates in a neighbouring tree from which another pigeon has been calling. On reaching its selected branch the pigeon's tail rises and falls in a rhythmic manner and the cooing begins anew.

The stock-dove's song can best be described in the following syllables: "Coo—*oo*—o. Coo—*oo*—o. Coo—*oo*—o." The calls commence softly working up to a crescendo and then fade away. The woodies' song consists of one call of "Coo—coo—coo—coo" and three or four calls of "Coo—*coo-oo*-coo—coo—coo", and ends on an abrupt "Coo". One can never confuse these two songs once they have been heard, as they are really quite different in character. The wood-pigeon's song is hoarser and more forceful than the smooth rendering of the stock-dove's, but both birds in their own different ways help to swell the woodland bird-song and form an integral part of the country scene.

THE FOOD AND HABITS OF PIGEONS

THE pig and the gannet are often referred to in humorous remarks concerning the eating of food! Though it can hardly be said that the pigeon is worthy of such notable company, it is nevertheless a fact that few greenstuffs, seeds and fruit seem to come amiss to the pigeon's digestion. The variety of food partaken is indeed extraordinary, and one can never be certain of what the examination of the contents of a pigeon's crop is going to reveal. Acorns and corn can usually be recognised by feeling the outside of the crops—as can greenstuff. Unless one knows where a pigeon has been feeding, however, a soft, bulging crop may contain anything from young clover leaves to cabbage and kale leaves.

Pigeons are perhaps more influenced by seasonal food supplies than many other birds, and I propose to list the main types of food available during the four seasons of the year. They are as follows:

Spring. Young leaves of clover, lucerne, sanfoin, etc.; spring sown corn—especially peas; green leaves of young peas and tares; young leaves of various trees—e.g. hawthorn; chickweed—leaves and seed.

Summer. Chickweed, grass seeds, young clover and lucerne, green peas and later seed peas, all forms of ripe corn and soft fruits depending on the locality.

Autumn. Barley, wheat and all forms of corn and weed seeds on stubbles; acorns and beech mast; autumn sown corn; young swede and turnip tops; berries of holly, hawthorn, etc.; chestnuts (sweet); rose hips.

Winter. All forms of greenstuff. In hard weather, cabbage, rape, savoys, kale, brussels-sprouts, kohlrabi, swedes, turnips, clover and lucerne; ivy berries; rotten potatoes.

It must be appreciated, however, that weather conditions affect the pigeon's feeding activities to a large extent, and thus, if a really cold spell is experienced during late autumn, for example, items such as kale, savoys and other large-leafed greenstuffs listed under winter foods will certainly be eaten.

The pigeon's food varies enormously from district to district: what does not vary is its hearty appetite. This remains constant at all times. As the grey light of dawn breaks in the east, so the pigeons get restless in the woods, and soon the first marauders are in flight towards some favoured feeding ground. During the summer months I have often heard pigeons beginning to "coo" in the woods before it has been light enough to make out nearby objects. This feed at dawn is maintained throughout the year. The other feeding times vary according to the length of daylight. During the summer months there appear to be roughly four main feeds: at dawn, just before midday, mid-afternoon and mid-evening. In the winter, when days are shortest, there are feeds at dawn, midday and late afternoon. Spring and autumn also have these three main feeds. There are always, of course, some pigeons feeding casually throughout the day in all seasons. During the breeding season there are hungry youngsters to be fed, and single birds and pairs will be constantly flighting to and from the feeding grounds. In the late autumn and winter, pigeons are much more dependent upon the length of day. Quite often, if undisturbed at their feeding ground, a flock of pigeons will spend the whole day in the same vicinity—especially if the weather is severe. When the nights are long and frosty, feeding is still most pronounced at dawn and late afternoon.

Once a good feeding ground is established, pigeons will continue to visit it regularly—often in increasing numbers —until they are disturbed, the food supply gives out, or a heavy fall of snow makes feeding impossible (e.g. clover and lucerne lays). Usually after a feed, pigeons will flight to some nearby wood or belt of trees in which to sit and digest their food—returning again as their appetites dictate. Thus, after a large flock has departed from, say, a field of clover, small parties of pigeons will begin flighting back again after a while to continue their feed.

On foggy days, when visibility rarely gets more than a hundred yards, flocks of pigeons do not often leave the vicinity of their roosting woods. They will feed on any suitable food to be found beneath the trees in the woods themselves or on adjoining fields. Fog is perhaps one of the pigeon's worst enemies—at least, as far as shooting is concerned—for it is possible to stalk within effective shooting range of a flock sitting in a tree without being spotted. Even after being shot at pigeons will seldom fly far in thick fog and will sometimes drop down into nearby trees. An approaching pigeon is easily detected by the whirring of its wings in the fog and more often than not it will be in range, for pigeons fly quite low in this weather.

Wood-pigeons are extremely fond of settling in trees before dropping down to the ground to feed. It will be noticed that preference is given to the tallest trees, for, above all, pigeons love to have a good view of the surrounding country in order to spot any danger approaching. A tree that is dead, or has some dead boughs near its summit, will be a favourite with pigeons, and it is surprising how frequently such a tree is used. I know of one such ancient oak which stands in a hedgerow on the edge of a small copse, well sprinkled with firs. The hedgerow is in one of the main flight-lines of pigeons approaching or departing from the wood, and this tree acts as a real draw to pigeons throughout the year. During the leafy months a few pigeons will often assemble about its bare branches prior to setting off to a feeding ground, and it seems such a tree offers a greater degree of security because of the good view afforded, than one thickly clustered with leaves.

When a flock of pigeons is busily feeding in a field, another flock will usually drop straight down with them without alighting in nearby trees and "sitting it out" for a while. There is often a continuous movement of birds among a large flock feeding, for instance, on a corn stubble, as the birds rise in ones and twos, flapping ahead of their companions in an effort to find better food. The reader will find that in many articles written on pigeon shooting the authors state that as pigeon's feed into the wind, decoys should also be placed head to wind. Pigeons do feed, normally, in the general direction of the wind, but mostly birds will be seen walking about in all directions. It is in my opinion far better to have decoys set out at various angles to each other, than all pointing religiously head to wind. Make the general direction of the decoys into the wind by all means—but do not have every decoy facing exactly head to wind. Remember that a feeding flock of pigeons turn into the wind ready for a quick departure if danger is nearby, hence it could be that approaching birds become wary of landing if they view such a "set" of decoys. (See Chapter 6.)

Hard weather—with plenty of snow and frost—makes pigeons less wary, as the urge to obtain food overcomes their normal instincts. The snow tends to limit their food supply and the severe cold increases their appetites. Even after much shooting and disturbance they will return again and again to the same patch of greenstuffs to try to appease their hunger. With the advent of milder weather—and consequently a better food supply—pigeons again become wild and unapproachable.

During the period when the deciduous trees are leafless, pigeons seem much more suspicious and alert than during the remainder of the year and shooting can be a very chancy business. For the most part they will be found feeding in flocks—sometimes running into thousands of birds—and it is relatively unusual to find many single pigeons flying about unless they are pricked birds.* Conversely, during late spring and summer when there is plenty of cover available in our fields and woodlands and the nesting season is in full swing, pigeon shooting can be somewhat easier and the birds more accommodating.

* Birds that have not been hit in a vital spot, but such as to make them feel sick and lose weight, are usually termed "pricked" birds.

★ 3 ★

MIGRATION

As the leaves of trees and hedgerows take on their autumnal hues and the acorns ripen and drop to the ground, the countryman becomes aware of the large flocks of wood-pigeons to be seen foraging in the woodlands and fields. Huge flocks may sometimes be seen winging their way to roost in the evening, their crops bulging with corn gleaned from the stubbles or beech mast found in some nearby parkland. One day there may be thousands of pigeons in an area: the next day—none. Such is the effect of migration on the pigeon population.

The migration of wood-pigeons is brought about, as in the case of other birds, by the exhaustion or inadequacy of food supplies in a given area—which in turn is also linked up with the climatic conditions prevailing. Flocks of pigeons will remain in a certain district providing there is a ready supply of food available. Once this food supply begins to dwindle in size, then the flocks will move on to another area where food is again plentiful. Similarly, if their feeding grounds become covered with a layer of snow such as to render feeding impossible and there is no alternative food in the area, pigeons will immediately migrate to fresh pastures.

Each year during the autumn and winter months the southern counties of England and East Anglia receive a great influx of migrant pigeons, and it has become a very debatable question, in recent years, as to the origin of these birds. Owing to the fact that so little is yet known about the migration of pigeons, there are still only theories on

24

the subject. Comparatively few wood-pigeons have been ringed in this country and on the Continent, and there is little concrete evidence available concerning the birds' movements. Of the relatively small number of recoveries of wood-pigeons ringed in Britain as nestlings during past years, the majority of birds have been recovered within thirty miles of where they were ringed, and there is only one record of a bird being recovered outside Britain, and that was found in France.

Flocks of pigeons have been known to roost overnight on the cliffs along our Channel coast and have flown out to sea on the following morning—only to turn back for land before getting out of the sight of binoculars. I have heard of only one instance of a flock actually flying completely out of sight over the sea. This has given rise to a theory which is held in some quarters that at one time pigeons did migrate regularly across the sea and that, although they do not migrate now, the urge to do so still exists.

I have even noted a cautiousness of leaving land shown by a large flock of pigeons flighting over the Blackwater estuary in Essex. This flock of about five hundred birds had flown for a mile over the water at a good height when, for no apparent reason, the birds suddenly bunched tighter together and rose much higher in the air. After turning a complete circle they once more set off on their original course. It could be that by gaining height the pigeons were able to get a better view of the land ahead and were satisfied that all was well.

Of wood-pigeons ringed on the Continent only one bird has to my knowledge been recovered in the British Isles. This pigeon was ringed in Jutland in 1925 and recovered —of all places—in Ireland in 1934. Until a far more extensive ringing programme can be undertaken both in the British Isles and on the Continent, the movements of the wood-pigeon will remain open to controversy.

There are three main theories at present concerning the origin of the large flocks of wood-pigeons that are to be seen in southern England during the autumn and winter months. Firstly, there is the theory that these flocks are simply composed of English pigeons which are always with us but which are more noticeable when in flocks. Throughout the summer months our resident wood-pigeons tend to be, in the main, split up into breeding pairs. One does, on occasions, see the odd flock of pigeons at this time of the year, but even so, on being disturbed, such a flock will usually split up into pairs, odd birds and smaller groups. In fact, a flock seen in the summer months on a feeding ground is gradually made up each day by the many pairs of wood-pigeons that flight in to feed. Hence, although a given area may hold a large population of breeding pigeons during the summer, this fact is not often appreciated by the layman—there being no quantity of birds on view together.

It is quite a different matter in the autumn and winter. Wood-pigeons are by nature gregarious birds and towards the end of the breeding season—usually about early October—they begin to form into flocks. At first, small parties of pigeons are much in evidence, the juvenile birds in many cases being still with their parents. As the weeks pass by, however, and the number of feeding grounds diminish as the stubbles go under the plough, so the small flocks join forces to form larger flocks, until by December there may be only two or three large flocks of anything from three hundred to one thousand birds each in an area.

As food is at a minimum in January and concentrated on fewer fields, the damage that these large flocks can cause is far more noticeable than in the summer months, when virtually the same number of pigeons are split up into pairs and have a plentiful food supply that can be obtained almost anywhere. On the face of it, this theory would appear quite feasible, although it is questionable whether there are sufficient numbers of resident pigeons in England to make up the flocks that ravage the countryside in winter.

Here is where the second theory on the subject could be the possible explanation to this point. This theory, which was advanced in a report by the Agricultural Research Council in 1951, entitled *The Wood Pigeon in Britain,* stated that a large population of wood-pigeons breed in the Highlands of Scotland, and that normally these birds migrate down the valleys to the lowlands, but that in a severe winter they do not stay in the lowlands but migrate to the south of England. It is also stated that juvenile birds migrate to a greater extent than the adults. The plumage of juvenile pigeons is dark slate-grey in colour during November to January as compared with the lighter grey of the adults. This fact would seem to tie up with this theory, for the large flocks of pigeons that winter in southern England do consist principally of small, dark-coloured birds.

However, I am personally very doubtful whether the Highlands of Scotland can support a very large breeding population of pigeons, as apart from the cultivated valleys there would not appear to be a sufficient food supply available. To support a dense breeding population of wood-pigeons a district must provide plenty of protein-rich foods such as corn and weed seeds. The Highlands of Scotland as a whole do not fulfil this condition, and although there may be pockets of high breeding density there must also be vast areas where no pigeons breed at all.

The third theory—and a much older one—is that many of the large flocks of pigeons consist of Continental migrants that have flown across the North Sea or the English Channel from Scandinavia, Belgium and France to spend the winter amidst our woodlands. This theory—

or should I say belief—is still held by many shooters and countrymen from Scotland, all down the east coast of England to East Anglia, but there is no concrete evidence either for or against the theory. Certainly, in Essex, there appears to be two main influxes of migrant pigeons. These usually occur between mid-November and early December and in January. The migrant pigeons or "foreigners", as the locals call them, are much smaller and darker in colour than our resident birds, and the white neck patches are not so prominent and in some cases are missing altogether. This is due, of course, to there being a high proportion of juvenile birds in the flocks. Whether it is a mild winter or a hard one does not appear to affect the number of birds to any appreciable extent, and this would seem to suggest that the birds do, in fact, come from the Continent, where the winters are consistently harder than ours. Another factor which I have noticed and which supports this view is that the large flocks of pigeons usually put in an appearance while an easterly wind is blowing—as with other continental migrants to these shores. It could well be that a certain amount of drift migration occurs—that is to say pigeons moving southwards down the west coast of Belgium may well get "drifted" across the North Sea on an east wind and finish up in Kent.

It can be argued that flocks of pigeons that have been seen coming in from over the North Sea in north Norfolk were migrating from Scotland and the north of England, or merely local flights across the Wash. However, when such a tremendous part of the migratory movements of birds is carried on during moonlight nights and the hours of darkness there is still much scope for this theory. Redwings flighting in from the North Sea during November nights can easily be recognised by their calls. Not so with wood-pigeons, for they give no call when on the wing.

Here, then, we have the three theories on this controversial subject. From whatever source the birds originate, however, there is certainly no doubt as to the large-scale movements of wood-pigeons that take place annually during the autumn and winter months in Britain. Whether the birds travel hundreds of miles or relatively small distances, the movement is still there. The habits of pigeons which are newly arrived in a district are different from the normal routine ways of the birds. New arrivals tend to be very suspicious and easily frightened. They will often fly around at a good height in the air during the early part of the morning as if afraid to drop in to feed—even though there may be plenty of food at hand. Usually they will take little notice of decoys and the bang of a gun seems to frighten them out of their wits. It is several days before they get into a normal flighting routine and use a feeding ground with any regularity.

All through the winter months these pigeons forage about our countryside obtaining whatever food is available. Quite often they are in time to assist our resident birds in clearing up the acorn crop in November. Autumn corn also gets their attention—as does beech mast and chestnuts (sweet) in the woodlands. Above all, however, it is the farmers' greenstuffs that suffer the worst damage from the hungry marauders. Cabbage, kale, brussels-sprouts, swedes, turnips, rape, savoys, clover and lucerne lays all share the punishment. The damage that can be caused by a flock of pigeons to a field of cabbages in snowy weather has to be seen to be believed. The birds settle on the actual plants themselves, and proceed to pluck at the hearts and young leaves. Eventually the cabbages take on the appearance of plants that have been attacked by a plague of caterpillars. The skeletons of leaves and the hard stalks of the cabbages are sometimes all that remains. Small wonder, then, that farmers and market gardeners are continually "up in arms" against the winged menace.

The departure of these large flocks of pigeons in late winter and early spring is not nearly as evident as their arrival. Here, again, much depends on the weather conditions and the food situation. When hard weather continues into March and sometimes early April, the return movement is delayed accordingly. As the spring sowing operations commence, however, and food is once more easily obtainable, so the large flocks become less numerous. Probably the flocks tend to split up into smaller units as more feeding grounds become available—that is to say the reverse procedure of the first theory on the subject. Nevertheless, I have noticed that in Essex we sometimes get a very lean period of shooting in April when few pigeons are evident in the district. This is certainly not due to the food supply—for there is always a plentiful supply of peas and clover available in the area—or the weather. This would again support the migration theories and suggest a return movement of pigeons.

Finally, the stage is reached in late April and May when the pigeons are once more in pairs—apart from a few flocks that have still to get the breeding urge—and the wanderings are over.

4

HIDES AND CAMOUFLAGE

FOR the young shot and beginner a hide ("blind", "hut" or "tent") may conjure up visions of a "wig-wam" type of structure situated in a field of corn to which pigeons are flighting in to feed. How very wrong. (Although I have noted such monstrosities on certain farms!) In very severe weather two or three poles with a couple of sacks draped around them may often be sufficient to conceal the shooter from hunger-stricken pigeon: in normal conditions the birds would take great pains to keep well clear of any such structure.

There are some pigeon shots who maintain that a hide is not necessary for pigeon shooting, and in some instances their reasoning is justified. For flighting pigeons in a strong wind (see Chapter 7), when the flight line may vary slightly with each party of birds, the restriction of a hide becomes obvious. Similarly, with pigeon flighting into roost a hide always has its limitations. For shooting over decoys, however, a hide is essential.

No matter where one is shooting, there are three main essentials that should always be borne in mind when constructing a pigeon-hide. They are:

(a) The hide should be large enough to give free manœuvrability to the shooter.

(b) The hide should blend naturally into its surroundings.

(c) It should be built—if possible—to give a good view of approaching pigeons.

If these conditions are rigidly observed the shooter should find himself making quite respectable bags—always provided he holds straight.

When I began pigeon shooting, the hides that I made were all composed of materials gathered from the hedgerows near the site—there being plenty of natural cover in the district. These hides served me well, although they did on occasions take quite a little time to build. Nowa-

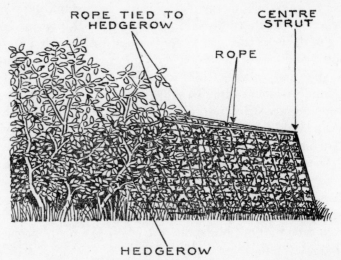

Fig. 1. The construction of a hide with a piece of camouflage netting.

days, I use a piece of camouflage netting (3-inch mesh) as the basis for all my hides. It has the advantages of being light to carry and quick to erect (saving hours of searching for suitable building materials). I have a piece of thin rope threaded through the top length of the mesh at one end, and all that is normally required to erect the net is to tie each end of rope to a convenient branch in a hedgerow, and have a stick acting as a strut in the centre of the net (see Figures 1 and 2). It is simplicity itself. Where there

Top : Equipment. A 12-bore automatic shotgun and cartridges ; two rubber pigeon decoys, at the bottom of the photograph one showing the spring and peg device ; a wooden pigeon decoy with small branch and string attached for lofting ; a silhouette decoy on the top right-hand corner of the groundsheet ; and a small haversack lying on top of a piece of camouflage netting.

Bottom : A hide built with natural material in a good, deep ditch.

Top : Making a hide with camouflage netting. Leafy branches and other hedgerow material will complete the hide. *Bottom :* A finished hide. Note centre strut supporting net, the rope along the top edge of the net, and leafy branches giving a better blend with the hedge.

are open fields and parkland—devoid of hedges and ditches—a piece of netting is a real boon. All that one needs to make a hide in such a spot are six stout sticks, preferably with a crutch at one end of each for holding up the netting and a sharp point at the other end for forcing into the ground. In woodland shooting the netting is also extremely effective and can be hung up almost anywhere to form a good hide.

HEDGEROW

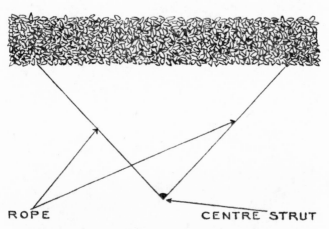

ROPE   CENTRE STRUT

Fig. 2.   Plan of the hide shown in Figure 1.

To enable the reader to become proficient in the building of hides, I propose to go into this matter in greater detail. The majority of pigeon-hides that are built are frequently only required for a few days' shooting on certain crops, and a change in the wind can even render a hide useless after one visit. Generally speaking ordinary pigeon-hides made from natural materials found near the site are quite easy to erect. The main thing to remember is that a hide should always blend naturally into its surroundings. When building a hide in a hedgerow (without a

3   33

ditch) several bushy sticks about one's own height should be obtained—if possible from the same hedge. These should be sharpened at the thicker end and forced almost vertically into the ground in the form of a semicircle so that the tops of the sticks point slightly inwards, with the hedge itself forming the rear of the hide. Some smaller branches from nearby trees, etc., can then be woven horizontally into the framework. Finally if the hedgerows are leafless—as they are during the best shooting months—

Fig. 3. A hide built with natural hedgerow materials. Note the "V" in the top front edge of the hide and the hedgerow background behind the shooter.

some dead bracken stems, thistles or grasses should be used to add the final touches to the hide. The rear of the hide should be higher than the front and sides, in order to give the shooter a background when he is standing upright. One must always avoid getting silhouetted against the skyline, for it is then that any movement is noticed by approaching pigeons. I usually make the front of a hide dip in slightly to form a "V" at the top rather than have the edge level (see Figure 3). This has the advantage of giving extra cover from and better observation of approaching birds, for one can look and shoot through the "V" without having one's head and shoulders fully exposed. When shooting over decoys (see Chapter 6) the front of the hide must be sufficiently low to enable the shooter to swing onto the birds flying low into the decoys —even if it means crouching down slightly until the birds are within range.

A really good hide should blend into a hedgerow so that it is not discernible to the naked eye, say, at 100 yards range. It is in late autumn, winter and spring that greater care must be taken when building hides. Nothing stands out more in a bare hedgerow than a hide camouflaged with dead, whitish grass taken from the hedge bottom. By all means use the grass on the lower part of the hide— where it looks natural—but remember to get somewhat darker materials and boughs for the top part of the hide. A few branches cut from an evergeen shrub (such as holly, fir, broom) are ideal at this time of the year—especially if such shrubs are plentiful in the neighbourhood.

Where ditches or dykes divide the fields, hide-building is simplified immensely. Providing that it has a good, firm bottom a ditch can be a real asset. It provides excellent natural cover for the shooter to the front and rear, and if it is of a good depth, only the two exposed "sides" need camouflaging, with perhaps some material across part of

35

the top of the "hide" if the ditch is too wide. For shooting over decoys when the birds are sweeping in low, such a hide can give the best of shooting.

There are many physical features throughout our countryside that offer almost natural hides for the shooter —and the more natural a hide is the better. The concave side of the high bank of a river, stream or gravel pit, or the hollow formed when a tree is uprooted in a storm are good examples. Farm crops can often be utilised as in the case of stooks of corn, bales of straw, partly used hay ricks and heaps of combine straw on the stubble. I have had some of my best day's shooting from a hide built on the underside of the high bank of a small stream. This stream flows through a small valley, and my hide was situated at a point almost equidistant between two large woods—both on the same side of the valley. The pigeons would flight to feed on the long field that ran alongside the stream and in which my hide was built. With a stiff breeze blowing down the valley, pigeons from one wood would follow the course of the stream in small flocks or singly and offer very good shooting. From the other wood they would come with the wind in their tails, high up, and go swirling past—finally to turn upwind to approach my set of decoys.

Where there are large fields or meadows, pigeons will often drop in to feed well away from any hedgerows or ditches. In such an event, a useful hide can soon be made, having first obtained permission from the farmer, by digging a small pit on that part of the field most used by the pigeons. If possible, it is best to dig such a pit a few days before going shooting, so as to allow the pigeons time to get used to the new feature in the field. The pit should be about 3–4 feet deep and large enough to allow the shooter plenty of room to swing a gun. The soil can be banked up around the hide—preferably higher to the rear of the shooter when facing the direction of approaching pigeons. Where possible, I always dig a pit on the side of a slope or depression in a field so that a background is formed by the slope itself. If the pit is dug amongst green-stuff, then camouflaged netting can be draped around the pit and supported by a few small sticks forced into the soil. Try to keep the top edges of the hide as near to ground level as possible, as pigeons are very suspicious birds and will usually avoid an isolated structure in an otherwise flat field. When there is little or no wind and the pigeons are approaching and dropping in from high up in the air, I usually camouflage the top rear half of the pit so that these high birds do not spot me.

At harvest time, when the pigeons are feeding on the fields of stooked wheat, the best form of hide is one made with a few sheafs of the corn itself—especially if the birds are pitching down far out from a convenient hedge or ditch. By arranging the sheafs into a semicircle with the "curve" facing the direction from which most pigeons are expected to come in to feed, a very comfortable hide can be built. Similarly, where pigeon are feeding on seed peas placed in large heaps on iron tripods to ripen, a hide can be built (after asking the farmer's consent) with a small bundle of the dry brown pea-bines. Bales and heaps of combine straw left on the stubbles awaiting collection can also be used to make good, natural hides. The whole idea is always to make a hide with the most natural material available.

In winter, when snow is covering the ground, an old white sheet draped around half a dozen sticks forced into the ground in a triangle or circle can make a very useful hide. Placed in a hedgerow or amongst standing kale it is ideal—especially if the shooter wears something white in colour to tone in with the hide.

Permanent pigeon-hides are sometimes erected amongst

the branches of suitable trees in the woodlands. The siting of such hides needs much thought and prior observation, for it is utterly useless to build a nice permanent hide only to discover later that very few pigeons flight over the spot. A tree-top hide should always be built in one of the main flight-lines into a wood, and must be a firm structure large enough to give the shooter adequate manœuvrability. Most of these hides are constructed of wood and are box-like in form—with a good ladder for ascending and descending. I personally have never used such a hide, but I believe that they offer excellent shooting when well situated—especially in dense larch or spruce woodlands. Generally speaking, however, a permanent hide built on the ground in a wood is quite sufficient for ambushing flighting pigeons. In fact some pigeon shots prefer no hide at all when shooting in a wood—a matter that will be fully dealt with in Chapter 8.

Where, for example, a meadow is frequented by pigeons year after year to feed on the young clover, a permanent hide may be very worth while, for you may depend on it that the pigeons will frequent the same trees every year. I have one such hide in a hedgerow beside a large elm tree, and each autumn I trim the new growth of hedge into shape in readiness for future use. The pigeons that have "met their Waterloo" when approaching that elm would certainly make a large flock!

Clothing worn for pigeon shooting should always be as sombre as possible. Something greenish for spring and summer and brown for autumn and winter is normally quite adequate. I find that ex-army paratroop camouflaged jackets or blouses are admirable—if they can be purchased fairly cheaply. "Anaraks" and similar Government surplus attire are also very effective. Old sports jackets are equally suitable—in fact any old clothing will do providing it is not too "loud". I never wear any expensive garment for pigeon shooting, for it is the simplest thing in the world to tear a hole in a jacket whilst climbing through a fence of barbed wire. After all, cartridges are quite expensive enough without having the additional cost of special clothing. A pair of corduroy trousers will be found to be very hard wearing and warm, but here again, any old pair of trousers (in reasonable condition at strategic places) will be sufficient.

Some form of headwear is really an essential for pigeon shooting, as a white face or sparsely vegetated head is so easily spotted by approaching pigeons. I personally wear a loose-fitting woollen Balaclava-helmet for most of the year—with the exception of very hot weather when I resort to a smaller woollen beret. With a loose-fitting Balaclava one can easily stretch the "chin" portion upwards to cover the bottom half of the face when pigeons are approaching. The top will also pull downwards over the forehead so that only the "eyes" section of the face is showing. Face-masks made of small mesh netting are worn by many shooters, and there is always grease paint for the dramatically minded. Whatever the method adopted, remember that it is still essential to raise a gun—or look around—unhurriedly. A quick movement, even though the shooter is well camouflaged, is often spotted by the pigeons.

Gloves can be worn in cold weather, especially if the pigeons are flighting infrequently. I always carry a pair with me all through the year, as they can be extremely useful when erecting a hide in a thorny hedgerow. For shooting and loading rapidly, however, I find that I am more proficient without them.

As regards footwear, I use a pair of Wellington boots (knee-length), unless the ground is very dry when I wear a pair of old shoes. Even so, in mid-summer, when everywhere is dry, the ditch in which you wish to build a hide will probably still contain an inch or two of water. I buy my Wellingtons one size too large—to allow me to wear two pairs of thick socks. It can be very cold waiting for pigeons in the winter.

I always maintain that the shooter who specialises in building good hides and camouflaging himself will make better bags (or at least have far more chances of making better bags) than the person who sets about his shooting in a casual manner. One must never underestimate the wariness of pigeons. The noise of a gun has a far less frightening effect on a flock of pigeons (in these days of continuous "rook scarers") than the glimpse of a shooter. A "bang" will often make the pigeons rise and circle around in the vicinity before landing again if no danger is in evidence: the sight of a man approaching is usually sufficient to put the birds in flight for some safer ground.

5

GUNS AND CARTRIDGES

Father: "There are some pigeons feeding on the peas on the eight acres. Take the 16-bore and see if you can get one."

Son (hardly believing his ears): "Can I really?"

Father: "Yes, of course, you are old enough to be able to use a gun now."

Such was my introduction to the shotgun just before my sixteenth birthday, on a fine July evening. As luck would have it, I did get a pigeon (quite a young bird) that remained a sitting target in an old elm tree after the main flock had departed. Not all shooters are as fortunate in having a gun provided like that at an early age. Hence a little advice on the type of guns and cartridges used for pigeon shooting seems desirable. Figures 4–7 show the

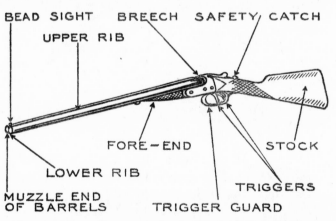

Fig. 4. The main parts of a double-barrelled shotgun.

41

main features of a gun and will be useful for reference later in this chapter.

The most popular gun in this country is the double-barrelled 12-bore, followed closely by the various smaller

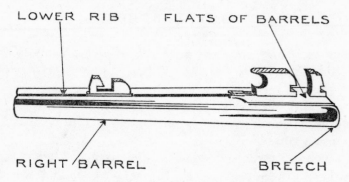

Fig. 5.   The underside and "flats" of the barrels of a double-barrelled shotgun.

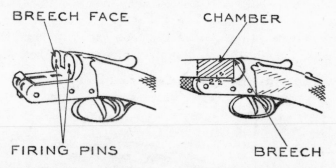

Fig. 6.   The breech face and firing-pins of a shotgun.

Fig. 7.   The chamber of a shotgun.

bores, namely the 16, 20 and 0·410. The word "bore" is a survival from the olden days when the size of a bore was based on the actual diameter of a ball of lead. A 12-bore, for instance, has a barrel bored to take a lead ball weighing $\frac{1}{12}$ lb., a 16-bore takes a lead ball weighing $\frac{1}{16}$ lb., and so on. Naturally, the killing range of the 0·410 is not nearly as great as that of the 12-bore, but providing that pigeons can be lured within effective range they can be killed in good numbers by this smaller weapon. The 16- and 20-bores are both extremely useful guns for pigeon shooting, and at ranges up to 35 yards are really on a par with the 12-bore. In these days of rising prices and purchase tax, however, not everyone can afford to purchase more than one gun, and the keen beginner would be well advised to obtain a 12-bore, hammerless, double or single-barrelled gun, if it is to be his "one and only". This is especially the case if rough shooting or wildfowling is also anticipated, for the extra few yards range afforded by this larger weapon may make all the difference between going home with something for the pot or empty-handed.

When purchasing a new gun, whatever the bore, there are three main points that need consideration:

(*a*) The weight of the gun.
(*b*) The size of chamber.
(*c*) The length of stock.

(*a*) A good class, double-barrelled, hammerless 12-bore chambered for 2½-inch cartridges should weigh approximately 6½ lb. A similar gun chambered for 2¾-inch or 3-inch cartridges will weigh about 7½ lb. The other smaller bores are all correspondingly lighter in weight. Single-barrelled guns are lighter than double-barrelled ones, although not appreciably so.

(*b*) As will be seen above, the weight of a gun is usually related to the size of chamber. If much wildfowling or rough shooting is expected, it is best to obtain a 12-bore gun with a 2¾-inch chamber so that a heavier cartridge can be fired giving a slightly longer killing range. Normal 2½-inch cartridges can always be used in a 2¾-inch chambered weapon for pigeon or game shooting. It is better to

buy a 2½-inch chambered gun—either 12-, 16- or 20-bore
—if pigeon and game shooting only are to be enjoyed. A
gun fitted with an ejector—for ejecting the spent cartridge
cases after firing—costs more than a non-ejector, and
unless one is likely to get much rapid firing a non-ejector
is quite sufficient for ordinary shooting. With this simple
mechanism there is less that can go wrong.

(c) It is wise to consult a recognised gunsmith about the
length of stock you need on your gun. This is in fact a most
important matter, for a gun should fit the shooter just as
snugly as a good lounge suit. Generally speaking a stock
is the correct length if one can "get onto" a target directly
the gun is brought up to the shoulder. If anything, the
stock should be on the short side to allow for the wearing
of more clothing in severe weather. If this makes the stock
too short for shooting in thin attire during the summer
months, a rubber recoil pad, which is fitted on to the end
of the stock, will adjust this.

If one cannot afford a new gun, it is often possible to
buy a good quality second-hand one through an advertise-
ment in a local newspaper. It often happens that someone
gives up shooting after a few years and decides to sell his
gun. He probably has no idea of current values and merely
asks for a sum which he considers is reasonable. That's
how bargains are obtained. However, I strongly advise
any would-be purchaser of a second-hand gun to check
on the following points most thoroughly before committing
himself:

(a) See that the gun has been nitro proved and that the
proof marks remain valid. Proof marks are usually made
on the flats of the barrels of a shotgun or otherwise on the
action or near the breech. British proof marks are made by
the London and Birmingham Proof Houses, and, in addition to these, the proof marks of certain foreign countries
are also valid in this country. Guns may validly bear proof

marks as required under the Rules of Proof of 1954, 1925 and, in some cases, even earlier. However, although a gun may bear proof marks its condition may have altered or deteriorated to such an extent since it was proved that it has become unproved at law and may well be highly dangerous to use. It is always advisable to consult a reputable gunsmith or dealer to ensure that a gun is in fact nitro proved and that it is still in a satisfactory condition before a purchase is made.

(*b*) Inspect the interior of the barrels for signs of pitting, dents or rust (always look down the barrels from each end in turn).

(*c*) Examine the outside of the barrels for dents, rusting or bulges.

(*d*) Examine the sides of the upper and lower ribs for signs of rusting.

(*e*) See that the action of the gun is not loose when closed.

(*f*) Ensure that the barrels are reasonably thick at the muzzle end. (A gun that has had much use often has very thin barrels—due to the great amount of cartridges fired over the years.)

If possible, ask the owner if you can borrow the gun for a day or two on trial. A gunsmith can always be consulted regarding the condition and value of a weapon, if one is not experienced in these matters, before any offer is made. When one is fully satisfied with the condition and performance of the gun, and the price is what one would expect to pay for such a weapon, then one can make the purchase.

As an aid to the shooter in his choice of weapons I propose to give a few notes on each of the guns mostly used for pigeon shooting:

The *12-bore* is a general-purpose gun, being the largest of the recognised sporting guns, and is widely used for driven game, rough shooting and wildfowling. It can be obtained as a double-barrelled gun (with either "side by side" or "under and over" barrels); as a single-barrelled automatic with a capacity for 2–5 cartridges; as a single-barrelled "pump action" gun holding from 2–5 cartridges; or simply as a single-barrelled gun.

The "side by side" double-barrelled 12-bore is still by far the most popular gun in this country and is ideal for pigeon shooting. As already mentioned, it can be chambered to fire 2½-, 2¾- or 3-inch cartridges. For pigeon shooting and everyday use the 2½-inch chambered gun is quite adequate, being slightly lighter in weight than the longer chambered guns—which is all to the good when swinging on to fast moving birds. The load for the standard 2½-inch cartridge is $1\frac{1}{16}$ ounces of shot. A slightly heavier load is obtained in the "maximum" cartridge ($1\frac{3}{16}$ ounces) which is also available for use in 2½-inch chambered guns. The standard load should be quite sufficient for pigeon shooting, and I never use anything heavier.

As regards boring, the majority of double-barrelled 12-bore guns are usually made with the right barrel bored "cylinder" or "improved cylinder" and the left barrel having some degree of "choke" (e.g. "half choke" or "full choke"). For the average shooter these borings are quite suitable. The term "cylinder" is given to a barrel that is practically the same diameter from end to end. "Improved cylinder", "full choke" and "half choke" are terms used for barrels that are narrower for the last 2 inches or so at the muzzle end. This narrow portion of the barrel is called the "cone" and a full choke cone gives a constriction of 0·035–0·040 inch. Half choke gives 0·015–0·020 inch and improved cylinder 0·003–0·005 inch. Thus a cylinder barrel, being almost the same diameter throughout, gives a good spread of shot and is very useful for close range work, whilst the various choke borings concentrate the shot—to a greater or lesser degree according to their constriction—and are excellent for shooting at longer ranges. The length of barrel normally varies between 25–30 inches, but I would recommend the shooter to confine his choice to a barrel length of 28–30 inches.

Regarding the spread or "pattern" of shot when a cartridge is fired from a 12-bore gun, it should be noted that at a distance of 40 yards (the standard range adopted for patterning shotguns) approximately 70% of the shot in a cartridge fired from a barrel bored full choke will strike within a 30-inch circle (the standard area). From a cylinder barrel there would be a pattern of 40%, and for improved cylinder, 50%. The greater the range over 40 yards, the thinner is the pattern.

The automatic and pump-action guns are also extremely useful weapons, but they do have the disadvantage of being rather heavy guns to handle—weighing in the region of 7½–8¼ lb. Nevertheless, they can be very good for pigeon shooting, and having more than two cartridges in one's gun can be a definite asset on occasions when the pigeons are coming in thickly—providing that one remains cool and unflurried. Most automatics on sale nowadays have a full choke barrel, although other borings can usually be obtained to order for no extra cost. For general pigeon shooting I would recommend an improved cylinder or quarter-choke boring.

In the event of a double-barrelled 12-bore being too expensive for the shooter to buy, I recommend him to get a single-barrelled gun. There are two or three reasonably priced models on the market that give first-class performances. One model is made so that attachments can be fitted to the muzzle end of the barrel giving various degrees of choke. These attachments allow one to adapt the gun to the type of shooting expected, and this can be extremely useful. Provision is made for a spare attachment to be carried in a special fitment in the fore-end of the gun. Here again, for general pigeon shooting, an improved cylinder or quarter-choke boring is recommended. A full-choke gun shoots much too tight a pattern for decoying when the pigeons are coming in close. Unless one is an expert shot, and can hit each bird well and truly in the head and neck, the bag may well look somewhat "shot-up", to say the least.

For the beginner, a single-barrelled weapon does cut down cartridge expenditure by eliminating the desire to fire a hurried second shot—as is usually the case with guns holding more than one cartridge. This is all to the good, for such necessarily long shots are seldom effective.

The *16-bore* is an excellent weapon for pigeon shooting, and for several years I used nothing else. Firing an only slightly smaller charge ($\frac{15}{16}$ ounce) than the 12-bore, it is to all intents and purposes the equal of the larger bore at normal ranges. Being lighter in weight, it has also the advantage of being less tiring for the shooter on a day when many cartridges are fired. There is no difference, however, in the cost of ammunition.

The *20-bore* is smaller again than the 16-bore, but is nevertheless quite suitable for pigeons—especially over decoys when the birds are pitching well in. Some "all-round" shooters do in fact use this gun for all their shooting. Here again, its lightness to handle is a great asset.

Finally, the *0·410* is the "baby" of modern shotguns (disregarding "garden"* guns). Its use for pigeon shooting is normally confined to shooting over decoys—when the birds are coming well in—and to shooting in young woodlands where the trees are only small. When pigeons are flighting low over the tops of trees about 20–30 feet in height a 0·410 really comes into its own. It has the advantage of being less noisy than the larger bores, and conse-

* No. 3 guns which are used for rats and sparrows, etc.

A woodland hide. The field of fire is restricted, but the hide is situated
in the centre of a good flight-line of pigeons.

Waiting in kale. Where the plants are tall a hide is not always necessary. The leaves at the bottom of the photograph have been eaten by
pigeons.

quently the disturbance created is correspondingly smaller.

Quite often the 0·410 is the first gun to be used by the young shot, and he should realise from the beginning that he is not the proud possessor of a miniature "ack-ack" gun or something similar. It is hopeless to blaze away at pigeons that one would be lucky to kill consistently with a 12-bore. The person who uses a 0·410 regularly, and nothing else, soon gets to know its limitations. When one has been using a 12- or 16-bore and then decides to try a few shots with a 0·410, one has the tendency to take shots at birds which are just that bit further off. Nothing is a greater sin in pigeon shooting than to fire at birds that are at extreme range—or even out of range. Not only does such shooting make the birds very wild, it also spoils the chances of other shooters in the vicinity. This is mostly true of organised shoots, of which more will be written in a later chapter.

Like any other craftsman's tools, a gun should always receive the utmost care and attention. A gun-cover or case is an essential for keeping or transporting one's gun when not in use, and I would recommend the shooter to obtain one or the other at the same time that he purchases his gun. Likewise, a set of cleaning rods and a small tin of gun oil are also essentials that must be obtained.

In the field, always make sure that when one leaves one's gun somewhere temporarily it is not in a position where it can fall down—or get knocked down—for the barrels of a gun are very easily dented if it accidentally falls on to a stone or roadway. The safest way of all is to lay the gun flat on the ground (*unloaded*, of course) so that it cannot fall down. One really bad habit of some shooters is that of standing their guns against the sides of their cars or propping them up in the back of a lorry or pick-up. Guns are expensive enough initially without having to pay for costly repairs.

Always make sure, when out shooting, that no obstruction in the form of mud, dead leaves or other matter gets into the barrels of one's gun. One cannot be too careful in this respect, as even a minor blockage may cause a barrel to burst—possibly with very severe or fatal consequences. I usually look through the barrels of my gun at regular intervals during a day's shooting just to make sure on this point. It is better to be safe than sorry.

On arrival home after a day's sport, the cleaning of one's gun should always get top priority. In fact, I make a habit of keeping an old piece of rag in my shooting bag so that I can give my gun a preliminary wipe-down, if it has been a wet day, before actually setting out for home. It is surprising how quickly a gun will get rusty after being exposed in wet weather, and it is always best to wipe it reasonably dry as soon as possible. The gun can then be given a really thorough clean at home.

On the question of safe gun-handling in the field, I cannot emphasise too strongly that one must always be extremely careful with a gun. The following points on safety may seem elementary to some readers of this book, but one still sees far too many reports of gun accidents in the press and other sporting publications that I feel there is no harm in stressing them again, especially for newcomers to the sport:

1. *Never* point your gun, whether loaded *or unloaded,* at anyone.

2. When out walking with a gun, see that it is always pointed either at the ground or well up into the air. Never carry a gun at an angle which will bring it into line with a friend.

3. When waiting for pigeons in a hide, do not stand the butt of the gun on the ground at your feet and rest your hands across the top of the barrels. You might be lucky

and escape with only the loss of a finger or two should the gun go off.

4. When getting through a hedge or crossing a ditch, always either

(*a*) remove the cartridges from your gun; or

(*b*) break the gun open at the breech.

Having the gun "on-safe" is simply not good enough.

5. Try to cultivate the habit of easing the safety-catch off "safe" as you bring the gun up to the shoulder to fire. This can easily be accomplished with a little practice and is far safer than keeping a gun "off-safe" for long periods.

6. Always make sure that your gun is unloaded when you have finished shooting for the day, or when stopping for a break during the proceedings.

7. When showing your gun to a friend always ensure that it is unloaded.

Purely as a precautionary measure, I would recommend the shooter to take out an Insurance Policy to cover any accident that may occur when using his gun. For a matter of ten shillings a year most insurance companies will issue such a policy to cover personal or third-party injury. For a slightly higher premium this policy can be extended to cover damage to, or loss of, one's gun. Considering the very good coverage afforded, this is certainly money well spent.

Finally, a gun licence must be obtained for your shotgun. These licences cost 10*s*. per year (expiring on 31st July) and may be obtained from any Post Office. If, however, you are also proposing to do some game shooting, a game licence, which costs £3 per year, should be obtained, for this also includes a gun licence. In other words, if you are the holder of a game licence, there is no need to obtain a gun licence. A game licence also expires on 31st July.

Cartridges containing various sizes of shot can be

obtained for any of the guns mentioned earlier in this chapter. Each size of shot has a number—the larger the shot, the smaller the number. Thus No. 1 shot is large, there being 100 pellets per ounce, whilst No. 8 shot has 450 pellets per ounce. For pigeon shooting it is advisable to choose a size between Nos. 5–7. I prefer No. 5 shot (220 pellets per ounce) and seldom use any other for pigeons. It gives a good pattern and has plenty of velocity and penetrative power. Birds hit at a good range in other than vital spots are much more likely to be gathered than those hit at the same range by sizes 6 or 7. Pigeons are strong flyers and will often carry on for some distance after being well and truly hit. I have found No. 6 shot quite good for shooting over decoys (and probably size 7 is equally as good) but for other occasions No. 5 is my choice. The slightly greater penetrative power afforded by No. 5's at ranges just in excess of 40 yards more than compensates for any loss in pattern density.

I cannot emphasise too strongly, however, that all shooters using 12-bore shotguns with standard load cartridges should regard 40 yards as being the maximum range for shots at pigeons. Over this distance the pattern of shot gets progressively weaker, and there is an increasing possibility of only slightly wounding one's quarry or of a complete miss.

Confidence in one's cartridges goes a long way towards successful shooting. Cartridges are often blamed for bad shooting, when the real fault is with the shooter himself. One does, on occasions, have "off-days"—when easy targets are missed. The man who has faith in his cartridges will as often as not realise his errors—perhaps he is shooting behind the birds or "poking" (not continuing his swing after the gun is fired)—and will try to correct them in subsequent shots. The man who has no confidence in his ammunition will tend to blame this, and further experiments with other brands will almost certainly take place in the near future.

My advice to beginners is to choose a well-known brand of cartridge and stick to it. Give each size of shot a good trial—for some guns seem to shoot a certain size of shot better than others—and then again, keep to the size you prefer. When you miss, you will know whom to blame.

There is at present a scheme in operation whereby Rabbit Clearance Societies are given a Government grant to subsidise the cost of cartridges used on behalf of their members for pigeon shooting. The Secretary of your local Rabbit Clearance Society or your local Pest Control Officer will give you details of this scheme as applied in your area.

PART 2

In the preceding chapters I have attempted to give the reader a general insight into and a "background" for pigeon shooting. I say, "general insight", because however much one reads on a given subject, there is always much to be learnt in practice. Books can never, unfortunately, make up entirely for practical experience.

The remainder of this book is devoted to the various methods of shooting pigeons, the main ones being briefly:

    (*a*) Shooting over decoys.
    (*b*) Flight-shooting.
    (*c*) Woodland-shooting at birds coming in to roost.

Other lesser methods such as stalking or driving feeding flocks, or calling pigeons can be (and are) employed, but bags are not nearly as large as those that can be obtained by the former methods. When pigeons do such a great amount of damage to farmers' crops each year, it is essential that shooters should kill as many as possible on every occasion. There is no question of leaving sufficient stock for next season (e.g. game shooting).

★ 6 ★

SHOOTING OVER DECOYS

WHETHER one is intent on viewing, trapping or killing a certain species of wild bird or animal there are two principle "draws" which make it possible to get on terms with ones' quarry: they are, namely, food and drink—with emphasis on the former. However wary a bird is in its natural surroundings, it has to eat and drink daily. Discover the food that this bird eats; where it is grown or obtained; and you can expect your quarry to put in an appearance sooner or later. In order to greatly increase the chances of getting a bird to come to a given feeding ground the use of lifelike decoys is often employed. Hence one of the most popular methods of shooting pigeons is by enticing them within range of the shooter with decoys. On paper this may seem a very simple task: in practice it is a very different matter.

To begin with, the shooter must set about obtaining some suitable decoys. There are several excellent types on the market today, although in my opinion there is no decoy to better a freshly killed pigeon when it has been properly set up in a life-like position (to be explained later). Nevertheless, one must have a few artificial decoys in order to obtain the dead birds.

In my early decoying days I had only two lifelike wooden decoys. Looking back, I realise that I did quite well in those circumstances. After I had shot the first two or three pigeons and had set them up with my artificials I found that the birds came in much easier. When birds are feeding well on a certain field two decoys are normally

57

quite adequate for obtaining one's first birds. If pigeons are not so keen on feeding, then the more artificial decoys one has to start with so much the better. I now regard four to six decoys as a a minimum for good decoying, whilst a dozen or more are ideal providing that they are light to carry. It is no joke having to carry about a dozen wooden decoys for a good distance to the feeding ground and then return with them after the shoot—plus the bag!

Gun-shops offer quite an impressive selection of rubber and canvas decoys nowadays, and most patterns do have the advantage of being light and are easily packed into a haversack.

Some types are fitted with a spring and peg device that allows them to move up and down when a good breeze is blowing—as if they are feeding birds. Another type can be fitted with rubber wings which can be made to "flap" by pulling on a line leading from the decoy to the hide. From my experience of some of these decoys there seems to be a tendency for them to be too dark in colour when compared with the live bird. I have even been to the trouble of repainting my wooden decoys in a lighter and more lifelike shade—for correct colouring is directly related to successful decoying.

During the long winter evenings the making of decoys at home can be a very interesting and useful hobby. One does not have to be very expert at woodwork in order to carve decoys from suitable blocks of wood—and the painting of them need not be too artistic. Diagrams with dimensions (Figures 8 and 9) are shown on page 59 for those readers anxious to try their skill. Wooden decoys have the advantage of being cheap to produce—the only materials required being the wood; two small black-headed screws (for the eyes); some turpentine and paints (white, black, blue and crimson will suffice); and a small dowel screw for fixing on the beak. A hole drilled into the underside of the decoy will enable a peg to be inserted for fixing into the ground—or a rod when the decoy is lofted into a tree.

Always use "flat" paints on decoys and never mix them with linseed oil, as this will leave a gloss finish that will shine brightly in the sun. I have, on occasions, watched pigeons approaching decoys that were shiny. All has gone

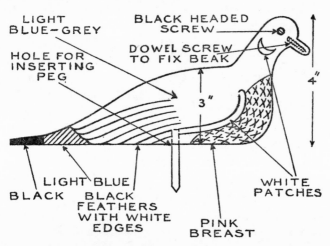

Fig. 8.   Dimensions and coloration of a wooden pigeon decoy.

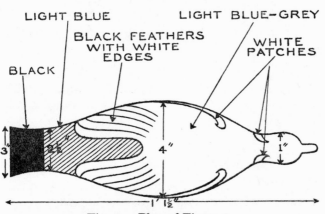

Fig. 9.   Plan of Figure 8.

well until the birds have reached an angle from which the shine could be seen—then their cautiousness has got the better of them and they have sheered off to flight to some alternative field. Not all birds sheer off, but a good number do—the number that makes all the difference between a fair and a moderate bag. If a decoy does tend to shine, a few gentle rubs with a piece of fine sandpaper will make the surface dull.

One of the best forms of artificial decoy is a stuffed bird. Taxidermy is not everyone's cup of tea, but it is really not so difficult as one might imagine. The finished article does not have to be perfect, as approaching pigeons are scarcely going to notice that a few feathers are out of place or that the legs of the decoy are partly made of wire! For cheapness in production and effectiveness in use a stuffed pigeon is hard to better. There are only two minor disadvantages with these decoys: firstly, they are only suitable for use in dry weather and secondly one needs to take more care when carrying them about. Although they are light enough to carry long distances, a wooden box, haversack or small travelling case is really necessary for their transportation in order not to damage the feathers.

For anyone who would like to try his hand at stuffing a pigeon, I propose to give a short account of the method I adopt.

The materials and tools required are as follows:

(*a*) A freshly killed pigeon with full plumage and free from blood stains or other damage to the feathers.

(*b*) A razor blade or sharp knife.

(*c*) A preservative for the skin. I use burnt alum with a dash of naphthalene flakes—both obtainable from any chemist's shop.

(*d*) Some ordinary corks—e.g. ex-wine bottles.

(*e*) Cotton wool.

(*f*) Some small lengths of wire, e.g. as used on small packing cases.

(*g*) A pair of pliers.

(*h*) A needle, thread and pair of scissors.

(*i*) Two small glass eyes.

Method

First make sure that the pigeon is not bleeding externally. If it is dribbling from the beak, stop this up with a

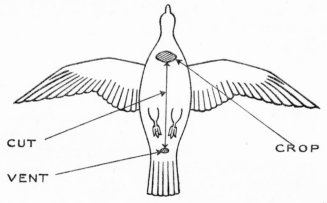

Fig. 10. A dead pigeon showing where to make the cut prior to skinning the bird.

small piece of cotton wool. Now with a razor blade or sharp knife cut the skin from the vent up the middle of the breast to just to the rear of the crop (Figure 10). Then gently push the skin back off each side of the breast; push each thigh through the skin in turn and cut the legs off at the joints thus leaving them connected to the skin. Push the skin back over the rump and back of the pigeon —do this very gently with the help of the razor blade where necessary so that the tail feathers keep intact with the skin, cut the wing-bones close to the body and pull the skin over the crop and neck up to the base of the skull.

61

Finally cut the neck off at base of the skull, and there you have your skin.

Next, remove the eyes of the pigeon and cut out the tongue. Use small pieces of cotton wool to absorb any blood. Scrape off any surplus flesh or fat remaining on the skin. Sprinkle the preservative liberally over all parts of the skin and put some into the eye cavities, beak and throat. Leave the skin for a day or two in order to let it dry out a little. It is then ready for the next stage.

In order to make the decoy stand naturally when finished the wire and cork are required. With the pliers, cut a piece of wire the length of the pigeon from head to tail. Push one end of the wire up through the neck of the skin and then firmly into the skull. Push the other end of the wire into one of the corks and thread the cork along the wire until it is almost halfway between the tail and head of the skin (Figure 11). Now bend the wire so that

Fig. 11. The skin of the dead pigeon showing the wire inserted in the skull of the bird and the cork threaded along the wire and in the centre of the skin.

the head and neck of the pigeon stand up in a natural attitude. The tail end of the wire can be bent round in an oblong to help form an internal frame for the skin (Figure 12).

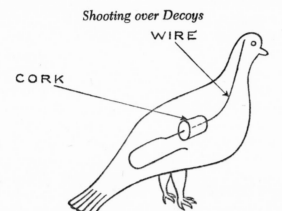

Fig. 12. The pigeon skin showing the wire bent into position.

Next, cut two lengths of wire sufficiently long to reach from the cork to the feet of the pigeon and still have about 6 inches to spare. Push one piece of wire down the inside of the skin of each leg and out again through the skin of the foot so that about 4 inches of wire protrudes from each foot. Then bend the top ends of the wires at right angles to the legs and push them into the rear end of the cork beside the main wire. Ensure that these wires are quite firmly fixed into the cork (see Figure 13).

All is now ready for the actual stuffing. From a roll of cotton wool pull off some small pieces and push them up inside the neck of the skin until it looks the correct shape and diameter. Then pack the front part of the breast using larger pieces of cotton wool. The needle and thread is now required to stitch up the skin of the breast as one works down the bird. Push cotton wool quite tightly around the centre cork to ensure that it keeps in position. Shape the skin as one goes along and see that it looks natural and not too bulky. Finish off the stitching at the vent.

The glass eyes can now be inserted, after first filling up any excess space in the eye cavity with a small piece of

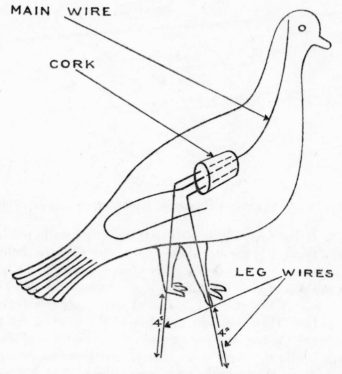

MAIN WIRE

CORK

LEG WIRES

4ˢ   4ˢ

Fig. 13. The stuffed pigeon showing the position of the leg wires in the cork.

cotton wool. If the eyes do not seem secure, a couple of stitches with the needle and thread to tighten the eyelid will usually do the trick. The wings can then be fixed to the body in a natural position by a few stitches through the wing flesh and into the side of the skin (Figure 14).

The decoy is now complete and ready for use. All that one needs do to set it up is to push the two wires, protruding from the feet, into the ground and ensure that the decoy stands naturally. In order to make the decoy easier to pack into a box or haversack, the feet wires can be bent parallel with the body and then reshaped when required.

Standing on a flight-line behind a thick hedge.

A dead pigeon set up on meadowland. A forked twig is holding up the bird's head. Clover, on which the birds were feeding, can be seen amongst the grass.

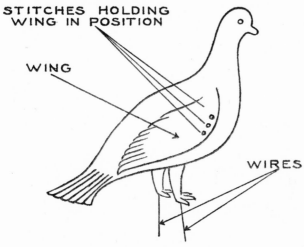

STITCHES HOLDING
WING IN POSITION

WING

WIRES

Fig. 14. The final product—showing where to stitch the wings
to the body of the bird.

By the above method a half-dozen stuffed decoys do not
take very long to produce, and their presence in the field
should quickly show ample rewards in the way of in-
creased bags of pigeons. I advise anyone really interested
in pigeon shooting to have a go at stuffing. One's first
attempt may not be all that is desired, but subsequent
birds will no doubt turn out first rate, and there is much
pleasure in using one's own creations.

As previously stated, dead birds take some beating when
they have been correctly set up, and the more that can be
put out the better the pigeons will come in to feed. It is
quite easy to "set-up" a dead bird in a lifelike position with
the aid of either (*a*) a small twig cut so that a crutch is left
at one end or (*b*) a twig sharpened to a point at one end.
The first method (*a*) is to press the twig into the ground in
front of the pigeon so that its head is held erect in the
crutch (see Figure 15). The alternative way (*b*) is to put the
pointed end of a stick in at the pigeon's mouth and then

5   65

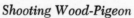

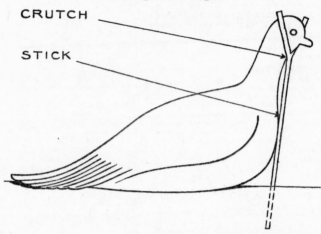

CRUTCH

STICK

Fig. 15.   A dead pigeon set up as a decoy with the aid of a small forked twig.

push it downwards so that the point comes out again at the bottom of the bird's crop. Then press the pointed end of the stick into the ground (Figure 16). Both these methods are very effective. There is one slight disadvantage with the first method in that the pigeon's head may get blown out of the crutch in a strong wind. I invariably

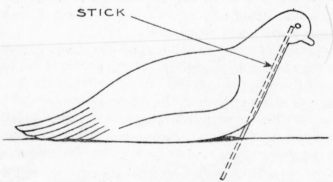

STICK

Fig. 16.   An alternative method of setting up a dead pigeon with a small, straight twig.

66

tear the eyelids off the dead birds before setting them up, so that their eyes are clearly visible. The feathers should be smoothed down, and any loosely hanging ones removed. The edges of the wings can be slightly raised above ground level by placing stones or clods of earth beneath them in order to show the white feathers more prominently. I usually set up the bird's head as high as possible so as to exhibit the white patches on the neck. When pigeons are coming in thick and fast one need not take such pains in setting-up the decoys, but when the birds are very wild, and few and far between, careful work is always worthwhile.

Decoys should be placed in position about 25 yards from one's hide—or nearer if desirable. I always try to site my hide in relation to where I intend placing my decoys. The closer to the hide one's decoys are placed, the greater are the chances of "rights and lefts" as the birds drop in. Whenever possible I build my hide so that the wind is blowing from behind me. This ensures that pigeons will come in towards me for landing. The decoys are set out facing the *general direction* of my hide (and wind) but *never all exactly "head to wind"* as advocated by many shooters. In my experience it is extremely rare to find a feeding flock facing *directly* into the wind—unless their suspicions have been aroused and they are preparing to depart. Pigeons tend to walk about and turn in all directions when feeding, even though the general movement may be into the wind. The more attractive and natural a group of decoys can be made to look, the less will be the suspicion of birds approaching to land. Three or four yards space between decoys is to be preferred—thus making the group as wide as possible. When one has, say, a dozen or more decoys in position, one can then set-out the next half-dozen dead birds in pairs whilst expanding the group still further.

When decoying pigeons and there is a strong wind blowing I usually place my decoys so that they face roughly into the wind and parallel to the hedge or ditch in which my hide is situated (see Figure 17). I then endeavour to kill one bird flying over the decoys and a second as the birds battle on against the wind. The first shot must not be taken until the birds are opposite—or just past—the hide, otherwise at the sound of the gun they will tend to scatter and depart downwind before another shot can be

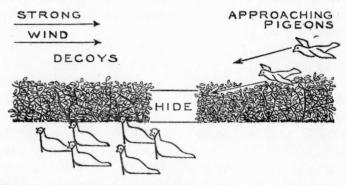

Fig. 17. The position of decoys in relation to a hide when a strong wind is blowing.

taken. When birds are coming in pairs to feed, the two birds are often quite some distance from each other when coming into land with the decoys. If this is the case, I let the first bird approach close in—sometimes it will actually land on the ground—before killing the second bird as it comes within range and then taking the other as it departs. In this way I get both birds instead of only one and thereby increase my bag.

The question of movement amongst decoys has raised a large amount of controversy in the past. Flighting pigeons are certainly attracted by a movement among their lifelike replicas—on occasions—but it is really the number of "still" decoys set out that catches their eyes. Hence the more decoys set-out the more birds are attracted. Aim to make the ground look really "blue" and pigeons will drop in without hesitation. After all, a flock of feeding pigeons is far more attractive to passing birds than just an odd bird or two.

Once I have plenty of dead birds set out, I normally take in my artificial decoys. The "set" should be as natural as possible. During lulls in the shooting I pick up or tread into the soil any loose feathers that may be lying about. If pigeons are coming continuously I leave the dead birds where they fall until there is a break in the flight. A "winged" bird or "runner" should be gathered at once—or else it may be lost—for pigeons can walk at a surprising speed. When one does leave the hide to pick up the slain always remember to be as quick as possible, for a figure walking about is far more frightening to approaching pigeons than the sight of a few of their comrades lying "toes upwards" on the ground.

Pigeons can be very disconcerting in their feeding habits, and it is always best to locate the part of a field that is being most "used" by the birds before building a hide. If there are any trees around the field, have a look on the ground under these for pigeons' "droppings". The amount of droppings under a tree is a good indication of how frequently the birds are using a field. Quite a lot depends, however, on the direction and strength of the wind. A sudden change in wind can quickly make pigeons use the opposite side of a field to that which they have been using for, say, the past week. This sort of thing can even happen whilst one is shooting, and the only thing to do then is to move with the birds and build a fresh hide.

The actual physical features of a field are often an important influence on the pigeons' feeding. A hollow or depression in a field—affording protection from the elements—is usually a sure feeding area for pigeons in rough, windy weather. Likewise, birds will feed under the lee of a thick hedge in similar conditions. In calm weather it is a different matter, and birds may well drop down anywhere in a field, especially if it is very large.

When approaching a feeding ground, wood-pigeons normally prefer to land in a tree before dropping down to the ground (stock-doves prefer to land directly on terra firma). Hence I always build my hide and site my decoys within easy range of a tree whenever possible. Otherwise, with decoys and hide placed about, for example, a hundred yards from a tree, birds will tend to sheer off from the decoys to land in this tree—and will often pass by out of range.

In really dry weather, I have found that pigeons will come into land on the ground with the decoys far easier than when it is wet and damp—when trees are preferred. The weather conditions do, in fact, have an appreciable effect on decoying. A layer of snow on the ground is funnily enough one of the worst conditions—when the layman would quite naturally expect good sport. This may be due to the fact that shooting is usually on crops of greenstuff (such as kale, cabbage, etc.) and the pigeons find difficulty in locating the decoys against the general background. The snow may even tend to dazzle them if the sun is shining. On the other hand, pigeons do get so hungry during a prolonged cold spell that they are glad to drop in anywhere to feed—without bothering to find their relations. (A case of "Blow you, Jack, I'm all right!")

Whatever the reason, decoying in snowy weather is certainly not very profitable, and it is far better to get on a flight-line or simply build a hide where the birds appear to be feeding most. Pigeons take little notice of a hide erected among the tall stalks of kale, and this is often the best policy when birds are pitching straight into feed. Use a few decoys by all means—but don't expect a great response.

At harvest time, when pigeons are feeding on wheat or other corn that has been "laid" by a storm or heavy rain, I set out my artificial decoys amongst the flattened corn on 3-foot canes (normally used in the garden). This gives approaching pigeons a better view of the "set" when the surrounding corn is high. The natural colour of the canes blends well with the golden stalks of wheat, and pigeons do not seem to care if the decoys are "sitting" a foot or so above the laid corn. The farmers' permission should always be obtained before setting out decoys amongst this uncut corn, and even then I walk in the crop as little and as carefully as possible. I attempt to shoot the pigeons so that they fall either on the laid corn or else in the hedge-row/ditch near my hide. It is senseless to shoot at birds that will fall well out amongst the standing corn, for searching for them would cause much more damage to a good crop (and it is usually the best and thickest crops that get laid). A farmer will not appreciate a shooter trampling down his corn still further in order to pick up a few dead pigeons.

Where corn is still cut by "binders" and the sheafs stood up in "stooks", decoys can be placed on top of these "stooks" within range of the hide. When setting up dead birds in these circumstances it is best to cut a long stick from the hedge (say about 2 feet) with a crutch at one end. The length of the stick ensures that it keeps rigid for holding the dead bird's head in position when the stick is thrust well into a sheaf of corn.

It is quite a common occurrence to see a flock of pigeons lift from a field where they have been feeding and re-settle on the next field if it is open. When shooting on crops such as turnips, swedes or laid corn, where it is difficult to display the decoys prominently, I have often used this

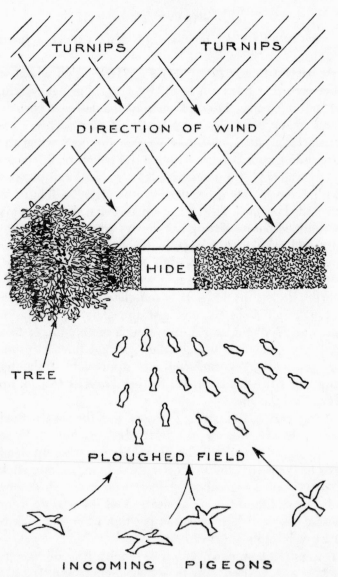

Fig. 18. Diagram showing the position of decoys on a bare, ploughed field when the crops on which the pigeons are feeding (turnips) does not allow the decoys to be seen clearly by the birds.

A small "set" of decoys. More dead birds can be set out as they are shot.

"Flaps-down" for landing. A pigeon coming into land with decoys—
one of which can be seen in the photograph.

A wooden decoy for lofting. Note the branch tied underneath the decoy, the string attached to the staple on its back and the lead weight on the other end of the string.

Lofting a decoy. The weight has been thrown over a bough and all
is ready for pulling the decoy into position.

habit to good advantage and made some large bags of pigeons by placing my decoys on a ploughed field or meadow where they have shown up plainly to approaching birds (as shown in Figure 18).

When the trees are bare in late autumn, winter, and early spring, I find that one or two artificial decoys lofted into the branches of a tree in addition to the decoys set out on the ground, give an added incentive to the pigeons to drop in to feed. It is quite a simple matter to loft a decoy into a tree with the aid of a good length of string and a lead weight—or even a stone. A wooden decoy is ideal for this purpose. A small staple should be driven into the back of the decoy so that when one end of the string is attached to this staple, the decoy hangs in a natural position. A small branch can be tied underneath the decoy (see Figure 19)

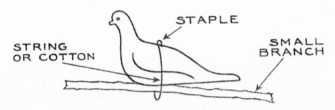

Fig. 19. A wooden pigeon decoy ready for lofting. Note the staple inserted in the back and the small branch tied underneath the decoy.

to give it a more realistic appearance, as one cannot perch the decoy on top of a branch by this method. The weight is attached to the other end of the string. To loft the bird, throw the weight over a convenient branch of the tree—preferably an outside branch—and pull the weighted end of the string until the decoy is in position just under the branch (see Figures 20 and 21). The weighted end of the string can then be fixed to a bush or other undergrowth on the ground. To get the decoy down again, untie the string

73

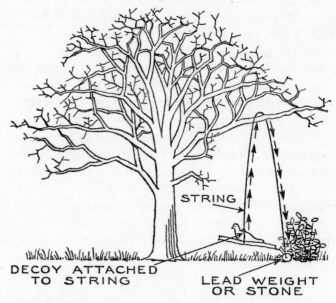

STRING

DECOY ATTACHED
TO STRING

LEAD WEIGHT
OR STONE

Fig. 20. How to loft a wooden decoy into a tree.

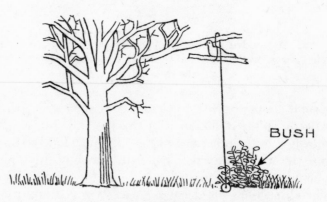

BUSH

Fig. 21. A lofted decoy in position. Note the weight and string
fastened to a bush.

from the bush and remove the weight. The decoy should then fall to the ground. If one has a long enough piece of string the decoy can of course be lowered to the ground.

An alternative method for lofting decoys into a tree is by the use of a set of rods, that screw together as per the chimney-sweep method. A disadvantage with the use of rods, however, is their extra bulk to carry in addition to one's normal equipment. The ball of string and small weight (as required for the first method of lofting) is far simpler altogether.

Apart from using decoys on farm crops or meadows where pigeons are feeding, a good place in the summer months is by a pond or cattle-drink in a river or stream. Pigeons like a drink of water in hot weather, and if decoys are placed naturally around a favoured pond, good sport can often be obtained. Providing that one can endure the aggravation caused by flies and insects—and the heat— two or three hours' shooting towards mid-day may yield quite a respectable bag. It is advisable to carry a finely woven sack or a large muslin bag in which to place the dead birds, to avoid them becoming "fly-blown". When a few of the slain are set up as decoys, a sprinkling of D.D.T. powder over their feathers and beaks will usually be sufficient to ward off the flies.

Coming now to the actual shooting of pigeons, when I first began pigeon-shooting all my birds were killed whilst they were sitting in a tree or on the ground, as I had yet to learn the art of shooting birds on the wing. I still shoot quite a few "sitters" in the course of a year—usually birds that have landed in a tree when I have been unable to see them approaching, or ones that I have stalked whilst they have been feeding on a field or resting in a tree.

To kill a sitting bird with a shotgun that gives a dense pattern of shot up to 40 yards range may seem all too easy to the layman. How very wrong! I soon discovered that sitting pigeons can be missed quite frequently unless one is very careful, for there is a fair degree of skill required. To aid the beginner, the following hints on shooting sitting pigeons may prove helpful:—

(*a*) Always hold the gun firmly into the shoulder and keep a firm grip of the barrels with the left hand (assuming that one mounts the gun to the right shoulder).

(*b*) Before shooting at a pigeon always ensure that at least one vital part of the bird is exposed. It is no good firing at the tail of a bird sitting in a tree if that is all that can be seen. The bird might lose a few feathers, but that would be all.

(*c*) Remember that even one or two small twigs between you and the pigeon can deflect the shot charge sufficiently to allow the bird to escape.

(*d*) When a pigeon is sitting in a tree and is not sufficiently visible for a shot, I call out a sharp "coo". This usually makes the bird look around for all it is worth to see what is wrong—often giving a much better target.

Many farm workers, labourers and countrymen cannot —or do not—shoot pigeons on the wing, but prefer to kill them when they are sitting targets, and often make good bags in this manner. From an economical point of view, when one considers the present cost of cartridges, this system is hard to better. I have a great admiration for these rural sportsmen who will go out in all weathers and often wait long hours for the chance of a few shots at pigeons. I am sure that they kill far more pigeons from their hides—be they in field or woodland—than are killed by the majority of shooters who attend the so-called organised pigeon shoots that take place annually in most counties during February and March. Therefore, if one cannot shoot pigeon in flight, by all means shoot them as sitting targets.

Hides for this type of shooting can be made in the

normal manner, but with the addition of a roof of branches or other vegetation further to conceal the shooter. If possible, the hide should be situated up-wind of a tree so that birds alighting amongst the branches of the tree will be facing the shooter—thus offering a better target. Do not take any notice of the advice given by some countrymen that one should always try to shoot at sitting pigeons from their rear, in the belief that the shot will have a better chance of penetrating their feathers. A pigeon is not nearly as tough as would be imagined from hearing pigeon-shooting discussed in the local pub. Providing that a pigeon is sitting within normal range of one's gun and that one's aim is true, there need be no doubt as to whether the pellets will penetrate its tightly feathered breast. They most certainly will.

Always remember to keep very still as the birds come into land and also move slowly when raising the gun for a shot. Pigeons have good eyesight and often detect a *quick* movement even through a well-built hide. It is best to wait for all the pigeons in a large flock to settle in a tree before firing, as often two or more birds may sit in line or close enough together to be killed with one shot. Do not, however, aim between two birds in the hope of getting both of them in the pattern of shot. You may be lucky, but usually both birds escape. Therefore, always aim at one bird so that there is at least the one addition to the bag. Shooting more than one bird with a single shot may sound unsporting, but where pigeons are concerned one must always bear in mind what a great pest they are to agriculture and market gardening. The more that can be killed, the less will be the damage to valuable crops.

Although there are books that explain how to shoot birds in flight and shooting schools that provide instruction in the art, many sportsmen, myself included, will have learnt the hard way. I did in fact graduate into shooting flying birds via shooting at running rabbits—and I expect this made things a little easier.

The occasion when I shot my first bird on the wing will always remain in my memory. What a red-letter day! I was walking along a hedgerow near my home on a fine September afternoon when a pigeon flew out low from the branches of a small oak tree. I fired at it just as it decided to twist over the hedge out of view—leaving a small bunch of feathers drifting in the air. Hurrying to a gap in the hedge, I was just in time to see the bird collapse in mid-air and drop beside the river on the far side of the next meadow. When I reached the bird it was quite dead and bleeding from the beak—probably having been hit in the lungs.

This initial success spurred me on to greater endeavour, and I began shooting at pigeons in flight as they came over my decoys. As I did not have permission to shoot at game or duck in those days, I had no chance of gaining confidence by hitting some of the easier targets afforded in some types of this shooting (e.g. the walked-up pheasant). But I did confine myself at first to shooting only at those birds that approached "head-on" or low—that is to say the easier (are they ever easy?) shots at pigeons. The birds that came in at other angles were allowed to land and were duly shot as "sitters". In this way I became quite proficient at one type of flying shot and doubtless saved many cartridges, and no little expense, in the process—for I was in no financial position to fire boxes of cartridges for no return in the form of saleable pigeons. Many keen beginners probably find themselves in this position today, and I strongly recommend them to adopt my system to begin with rather than attempt shooting at every conceivable pigeon within range. Being able to kill pigeons fairly consistently at a certain angle of flight boosts one's morale enormously and gives one plenty of spirit to try the more difficult shots in due course.

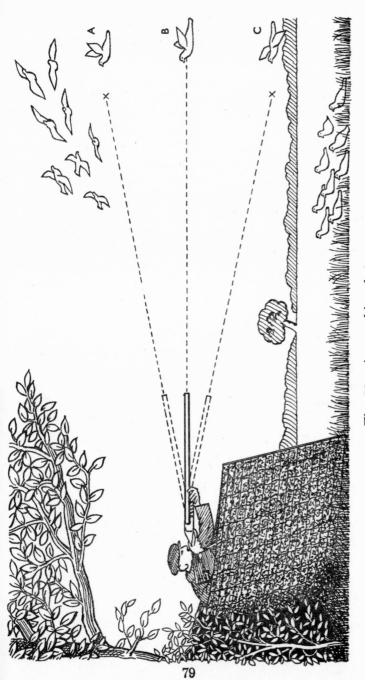

Fig. 22.   Approaching shots.

For the benefit of those who are keen to shoot pigeons on the wing, the diagrams on pages 79–84 may be of some assistance.

The pigeon marked "A" in Figure 22 is approaching directly towards the shooter and just above the level of his head. Providing its flight remains straight all that one needs do to kill such a bird is to bring the gun up to the shoulder, aim at the bird and at the moment of firing lift the muzzles slightly so as to "blot out" the bird from one's vision. Perhaps I should not really use the word "aim" in connection with shooting at moving targets, for with the majority of shots it is best to forget all about the little bead sight at the muzzle end of the barrels. It has to be realised that as the pigeon will be moving all the time, one only points the gun momentarily at the bird. Pigeons frequently change their direction and angle of flight, and it is not advisable to bring the gun up to the shoulder too early. There is always the tendency to do this when a pigeon has been watched approaching for a good distance. This often results in a clean miss—due to the shooter dwelling too long over the shot and the pigeon changing its course. The best policy, therefore, is to wait until the bird gets within easy range then raise the gun and fire directly it comes into the shoulder.

Pigeon "B" is a direct head-on shot and necessitates firing directly at its head and breast. This type of shot should not be missed, but here again a bird that is flying head-on at one moment can suddenly glide lower or swerve to left or right—thus avoiding the pattern of shot. Pigeons rarely fly at the same angle of flight for any distance, and the shooter that hesitates over his shots will find that he is missing far more birds than he should do.

When shooting at a low-flying pigeon—"C"—shoot below or under the bird (i.e. in front of it) otherwise the shot will pass over the top of (or behind) the bird.

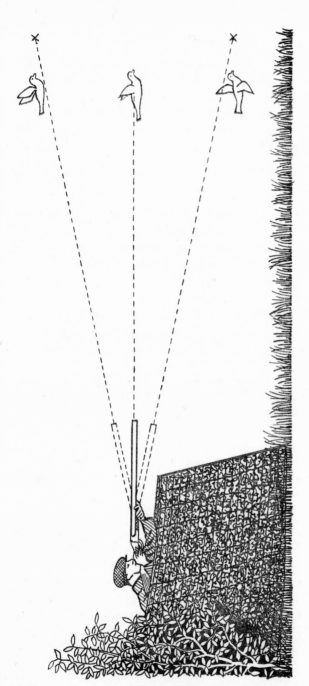

Fig. 23. "Going-away" shots. For the top bird the gun must be swung through and under (i.e. in front of) the bird. The centre bird is a straightforward going-away shot at eye level, whilst to kill the bottom low-flying bird the shooter must shoot over, and likewise in front of, the quarry.

After I had graduated at these three types of shot I became more ambitious, and the next types of shot I developed were the "going away", "crossing" and "quartering" varieties—as shown in Figures 23, 24 and 25 respec-

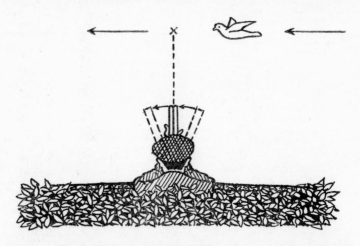

Fig. 24. The crossing shot. For this shot one must assess the speed of the bird and then swing the gun through and well ahead of the bird—continuing the swing of the gun as the trigger is pulled.

tively. In fact I was fast beginning to gain confidence in killing pigeons on the wing. The overhead shot (Figure 26) was my crowning achievement.

There are, of course, many other variations in the flight of pigeons that are mastered only after much experience in the field. Each bird needs to be taken on its merits— and there is no time for slide-rule calculations! In my early shooting days I tended to be perhaps a little too quick in firing my gun, and although my shooting was fairly good there were often occasions when a less hasty shot would have paid better dividends. In any case I certainly had my full share of "misses" during my early years.

I can well remember one morning in June when I shot sixteen times for five pigeons. At the time I considered my shooting was awful, but since then I have realised that as a beginner I really did quite well. Similarly, on a bitter winter's day in February, with the wind blowing "half a gale", I shot many cartridges for a mere three "blue rocks"

Fig. 25. The quartering shot. This is a shot taken when the bird is at an angle between the crossing bird and the bird flying directly away from the shooter. The necessary allowance in front of the bird decreases as the bird nears the straight-away angle.

Fig. 26. The overhead shot. Wait until the bird is nearly overhead, then swing the gun well through and ahead of the bird, the
body being thrown back so that the weight is on the right leg.

as they flighted into feed on a field strewn with rotting potatoes.

As in other sports, regular practice in the field is vital if one wishes to become a good shot. That is why some of the finest all-round shots in this country are gamekeepers —who are continually in action throughout the year. Shooting pigeons in flight over decoys provides a beginner with an excellent foundation to all forms of shooting. In fact, when the shooter reaches the stage of killing "rights and lefts" (i.e. one bird with each barrel) regularly, he should have no doubts as to his ability to aquit himself satisfactorily at driven or walked-up game and at wild-fowling.

However, even when a shooter considers himself quite proficient, there will be days when the empty cartridge cases lying in the hide will be numerous but the bag small. This happens to most of us. Shots that are normally regarded as "certainties" are missed—the reason? . . . Who can say? Cartridges often get the blame: sometimes the gun. But usually it is the fault of the shooter himself. A good shot has a pretty good idea as the trigger is pulled whether he has hit or missed his quarry. If he misses the bird, he usually knows why. Insufficient lead in front of a bird is, I suppose, the most prevalent reason for misses. "Poking"—or failing to continue swinging the gun and "following through" as the trigger is pulled—is another. One should always remember that in shooting every movement of the gun must be smooth and calculated. Just as a good cricketer can crack a ball through the covers with apparent ease, so the good shot will "pull" down a high bird with a casualness that gives the "I think I could have done that" idea to the layman. How often does a skilled job look easy when it is well performed.

★ 7 ★

FLIGHT-SHOOTING

ANYONE who makes a careful study of the habits of pigeons will soon notice that once a feeding ground is established many birds approach the field from the same direction and usually fly along quite a definite route. Exactly the same thing happens with pigeons approaching or departing from a large wood, or, for that matter, even a small spinney. The birds may, for example, follow the line of a hedgerow or flight along the shoulder or brow of a small valley; they may flight across open farmland and invariably pass over a small, isolated bunch of willow trees or close to a solitary oak. In the shooting world such a route is generally known as a flight-line, and often the shooting afforded by pigeons using such a line can be first-class.

Flight-shooting, as the name implies, normally means the interception and shooting of birds on their regular flights from one place to another. Just as one gets the same numbered Corporation bus, using the same route, to get to the town centre for shopping, so a pigeon will fly over a certain route each time in order to get to its feeding ground. The flight-lines used by pigeons are usually found to be from woodlands to feeding grounds and vice versa; from one feeding ground to another; or between two woodlands. There are, in fact, really two types of flight-line, which I propose to call permanent and temporary lines.

Permanent flight-lines are often quite short in length—perhaps only 200 yards or half a mile—and are usually found on the outskirts of woodlands. These flight-lines will

86

be found to be used regularly, according to the direction of the wind, whenever pigeons are in the area. Quite often the birds will flight out of or into a woodland along a hedgerow which links up with the woodland itself. This is especially the case where a hedgerow has several trees along its course, for pigeons prefer to flight over trees, or in the lee of them, whenever possible.

Temporary flight-lines are usually found *en route* between woodlands and feeding grounds and, on occasions, between one feeding ground and another. The latter flights may occur when a feeding ground is being disturbed in some way and the birds are forced to seek an alternative field. Unlike permanent flight-lines, temporary lines are far more uncertain and may only be in use for a few days —or even hours. On the other hand, they may be used for several weeks whilst the food supply remains plentiful. One can anticipate a good day's sport on the morrow— allowing for the direction and strength of the wind (perhaps based on the B.B.C. weather forecast)—and then find on arriving at the venue that there is little or no wind, its direction has changed and the birds are few and flying extremely high. On other occasions when one sets out with only a small number of cartridges on the off-chance of a shot or two, the pigeons will be found flighting low and continuously into a strong breeze that has suddenly sprung up. Needless to say the cartridges are used in no time, and one is left wondering as to what the bag might have been if one had brought sufficient ammunition. It was ever thus!

A flight-line on one side of a wood is usually only good for certain directions of wind—as is illustrated in Figure 27.

In this example, the hide in question would probably be useful only on days when westerly or easterly winds (or slight variations thereof) were blowing. The former wind would keep pigeons approaching the wood reasonably low and in range, whilst the latter would be blowing against pigeons flighting outwards from the wood. Pigeons will sometimes fly low with the wind, but more often they will pass over too high to offer any shooting.

One should always be prepared to move one's position according to the flights of pigeons. This does not mean that I advocate moving a hide if two or three flights pass by wide and out of range, but if several birds flight wide, then one must review the situation. Sometimes moving a hide 10 yards further along a hedgerow will enable one to keep in the main flight-line of the birds. Another useful

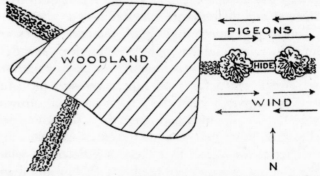

Fig. 27.   The siting of a hide on a flight-line in a hedgerow outside a woodland.

method to adopt when pigeons are flighting just wide on either side of one's hide is to hang up some large pieces of white newspaper or rag on the hedgerow or fence about 100 yards away on each side of the hide. This tends to make these birds converge into range.

When pigeons are flighting very low and there is a thick hedge of medium height, allowing one to see approaching birds at a distance, or an open ditch to conceal one from the birds, I usually dispense with a hide. This enables me to walk (or run) along under cover to intercept flights of pigeons which would pass wide of my position. This method often proves very satisfactory, but on some occa-

sions it can backfire, for after anticipating where a flight
of birds will cross the hedge, one moves quickly to that
spot only to find that the birds have changed course and
are just passing over one's original position. Small wonder
that the air suddenly gets blue!

A few decoys placed on open ground in full view of
the flighting pigeons is also a useful method to employ,
and I have made many good bags in this way. Decoys are
perhaps the best way of making pigeons, which would
otherwise pass by out of range, converge over one's hide.
Similarly, when birds are flighting over high in the air, the
decoys will often lure them down within range.

Whenever possible, it is always best to make a hide well
away from either end of a flight-line, for once pigeons are
seriously disturbed at a feeding ground—or where they
rest—a flight-line will peter out. Pigeons will not, under
normal weather conditions, tolerate any lengthy persecution when there are plenty of quieter spots in the vicinity.

The duration of pigeon flights varies enormously from
day to day. Sometimes the pigeons will flight on and off
all day long whilst on other occasions the flight may last
for an hour and then stop abruptly. Dawn is possibly the
only time when flighting can be fairly certain, and then
only when weather conditions are correct. Pigeons start
flighting out from their roosting woods soon after dawn
breaks. This is particularly the case in winter when the
nights are long and cold and food is not too plentiful.
Often the birds will fly in large flocks, and with a strong
wind blowing against them these flocks may stretch out
for half a mile or more. When one is shooting near a woodland the main dawn flight usually only lasts until the
pigeons have all set off for their feeding grounds. If one
is fortunate enough to be nearer a feeding ground, one
may get far more shooting as birds converge on to the
flight-line from other woodlands.

I have often noticed that pigeons always tend to flight out of woodlands into a strong wind and that feeding grounds upwind of a wood are used more frequently than those downwind whilst the strength and direction of the wind is maintained. This is provided that there are plenty of feeding grounds in the area.

Besides flighting to obtain food, pigeons will also flight to get a drink in hot, dry weather. During one exceptionally hot summer there was a continuous flight of pigeons to one of my local reservoirs. This flight was probably brought about by the fact that most of the small ponds and ditches in the area dried up completely during the weeks of hot weather and the reservoir became the main drinking place for most pigeons in the vicinity. Such conditions are, of course, very exceptional—for we may not get another summer such as that for many years. Nevertheless, pigeons do flight regularly to ponds, rivers and streams to get a drink in hot weather and quite reasonable bags can sometimes be made.

For actual sporting shots, flight-shooting at pigeons is hard to better, for it can beat covert shooting and other driving all ends up in the variety of shots provided. Indeed, I often wonder if sportsmen who do little or no pigeon-shooting really know how much they are missing. Often known as "the poor man's pheasant", the wood-pigeon certainly lives up to this description, and remains a constant source of sport throughout the year.

8

WOODLAND-SHOOTING AND ORGANISED
PIGEON SHOOTS

WHEN the woodlands stand cold and bleak in the grip of winter and frost glistens whitely on the dark green foliage of the spruce trees, then is the time to enjoy pigeon-shooting as the birds flight into roost in the late afternoon, against a grey, snow-threatening sky. This type of sport can often provide some of the best shooting obtainable during the year. To kill a small bag of moderately high birds as they are coming in to roost will give one far more satisfaction than the score or so easier shots at game when out with the syndicate. These are the shots that remain in the memory.

Let it not be imagined, however, that all the shooting will be at high birds. The type of terrain and the height of the trees usually dictate the height at which the pigeons will be shot. The most important thing to remember is that the birds must be allowed to make their final approach into land before any shooting takes place. In this way it is possible to kill far more birds and allow more shooting at the large flocks. Where only a single shot would be possible at a flock circling high in the air, two, three or even more shots can be managed when a similar flock is flying low.

When taking up a position for shooting in a wood one should always try to anticipate where the most profitable "stand" will be. The direction and strength of the wind are important factors to bear in mind. Flocks of pigeon will usually alight into the wind—even though the approach may be fast downwind. In a really strong wind, the birds will probably come in low and settle directly into the trees on the lee-side of a wood. In this event shooting can be enjoyed from a hide built on the edge of the wood, the birds being taken well out in front—at times almost like driven grouse. When the wind is light it is a very different proposition. Flocks of pigeons will often appear very high above the wood, circle lower until they are satisfied that everything is peaceful, then set their wings and drop into the trees. On other occasions, especially if a few pigeons are already sitting in the wood, a flock will glide on set wings and drop straight in—when the swishing sound of their wings is sometimes the first indication the shooter has of their approach.

On these calm evenings, pigeons have a habit of landing first of all in the tallest trees of a wood, before fluttering down into the smaller trees and shrubs when they feel secure. I usually select a spot for a hide just downwind of some tall trees on such evenings, otherwise birds dropping into these trees may well pass over too high for shooting —or at least for making a reasonable bag.

When a woodland is composed of small trees—as in young larch and spruce plantations—pigeons will often alight in taller trees in the vicinity of the wood prior to flighting into the wood to their final roosting site. This habit can be turned to good account if a hide is made near such a tree and occupied for the earlier part of the evening —the shooter proceeding to the wood just before dark to await the final roosting flight. Actually, in organised shoots, it often pays to have a gun stationed in any large clumps of trees outside the woods, for pigeons will usually pitch into these if shooting is going on in the woods.

The degree of alertness of pigeons flighting into roost depends mostly on the weather conditions and the amount of persecution they have suffered in the neighbourhood.

In severe weather, when it is freezing hard or a bitter wind is blowing, pigeons will drop straight into a wood without prior reconnaissance.

On one such occasion, in early February, the weather had been very cold with an easterly wind blowing for several days but little snow. I arrived at a small covert about 4 p.m. to find several pigeons already sitting in the row of scots pines that lined one side of the middle ride. The covert was situated on one side of a small valley and I quickly erected a hide, with the aid of my piece of camouflage netting, on the edge of the ride with the wind blowing from the rear. The bottom half of the covert sloped away before me, and pigeons were soon flighting in low across the ride. Each time I fired other pigeons would get up below me and flight straight over me into the top half of the wood. I shot twenty-one in the short time before darkness fell and thoroughly enjoyed the sport— even forgetting that my feet were very cold.

Mild weather, on the other hand, coupled with shooting and disturbance in the area, will make the birds extremely wary. Flocks will circle over the woodlands time after time before landing. Stock-doves are particularly prone to this habit, and have a much quicker eye for danger than the "woodie". They will flight fast and low over the trees seeming to search every part of the wood in their path.

Pigeons flighting low over woodland have a habit of avoiding large gaps and clearings in the trees. It will be found that flight-lines often pass over the thickest parts of a wood. Thus, although a hide built in a large clearing may give one a large firing area, it is utterly useless if birds are passing wide and out of range over the trees. A good site for a hide is often to be found on the edge of a narrow ride or in a small gap in a belt of trees over which the birds are flighting. One can usually tell which part of a wood has been most used by the pigeons, by the amount of droppings on the ground under the trees. It is not always profitable to make a hide amongst these trees, however, for the pigeons will probably settle in another part of the wood first of all, before fluttering down to roost for the night. It is far better to place oneself so that birds that are approaching to land can be intercepted.

Where possible, pigeons prefer a sheltered spot for their roost, and certain woods are far more attractive than others in this respect. Woodlands growing on the slopes of small valleys offer perhaps the best shelter from the elements, especially if some conifers are present, the leeward side of a valley being most tenanted. Pigeons do not appreciate undue disturbance at their roost and regular shooting will make them seek quieter coverts. It is unwise, therefore, to shoot the same wood too frequently if good bags are to be obtained. Far better, under normal weather conditions, to go once a week and have a good evening's sport. If the weather is severe, then, as explained earlier, pigeon are less wary and more frequent visits can be made. (Always providing that one is fortunate enough to get away from work *and* the wife!)

There has been much controversy in the past over the method of camouflage to be adopted when shooting pigeons in a wood. Some shooters maintain that a hide is unnecessary: others swear by one. I am inclined to reach a happy mean. Under normal weather conditions I choose a convenient spot—either from local knowledge of the wood or after watching a few flights of pigeons coming in —and erect my triangular hide with the aid of my piece of camouflage netting (see Figure 1). When one is shooting at pigeons flighting in over tallish trees, it is best to have the netting sloping inwards at an angle of about 70° with the ground so that one can stand under the net and be able to shoot at birds passing overhead—for low shots are unlikely. In this way it is possible to get a maximum of shooting with a minimum of movement—the ideal to achieve when shooting in woodlands.

Coupled with my hide I wear my grey woollen Balaclava-helmet which is quite loosely fitting and enables me to pull the "chin" section upwards over my mouth and nose if desired, so that only part of my face and my eyes are showing. I do not wear clothing that is too dark, as this only tends to make a sharp contrast with one's hands and face when viewed from above. Pigeons will veer away at the sight of a white face amongst the trees—even though the shooter is stationary.

Remember to stop shooting in a wood before it is quite dark, so that any pheasants are able to go up to roost in peace. If other guns are shooting in the same wood, don't go wandering about looking for an odd bird that may have been hit. Above all, be courteous to your host and offer him a brace or two of the bag. It may not seem much in the way of payment for the sport enjoyed, but it is appreciated, and when the time comes for another shoot an invitation will be assured.

Organised pigeon shoots are conducted in most counties where pigeons abound after the close of the game-shooting seasons. The organisation of these shoots is usually handled by the County Agricultural Executive Committees through their local Pest Control Officers. Farmers and landowners are notified of the dates of the shoots, often through the local press, and are requested to have their woodlands manned, on the days in question, as the pigeons flight in to roost in the late afternoon and evening. In Essex, for example, shoots take place on Saturday afternoons during February and March when an attempt is made to have one or more guns stationed in each woodland and spinney throughout the area. The theory behind these shoots is that larger bags of pigeons can be made if the pigeons are kept on the move from wood to wood and not allowed any sanctuary.

Good results are often achieved by these large shoots, but I feel sure that if only some shooters would refrain from being "trigger-happy" the results could be far better. It is difficult enough for an experienced shooter to kill pigeons regularly as they flight over woodland, and near impossible for the novice. Pigeons are often fired at by inexperienced shots when they are far too high in the air to warrant a shot, and this tends to make the birds more wary than usual.

It may not normally be sporting to shoot sitting birds, but at this type of shoot sport is the last thing to be considered. It is the total bag of pigeons that matters, and I would seriously recommend anyone who cannot shoot birds reasonably well on the wing to allow the pigeons to land in the trees before firing. An organised shoot is *not* the time to get in some practice at flying birds.

An essential point to remember when one has promised to take part in an organised shoot is that if for some unforeseen reason one cannot turn up for the shoot, always advise the organiser beforehand or find oneself a replacement. To leave a wood without a gun during an organised shoot gives the pigeons a nice quiet sanctuary and defeats the object of the shoot.

I often feel that another method of organised shooting would pay far better dividends than shooting the birds at their roosting grounds. This method would be to shoot the pigeons over decoys at their feeding grounds, and also on their flight-lines, on pre-arranged days or half-days over a large area. In actual fact, this type of shooting does take place unintentionally on some weekends, when independent shooters are out on several farms in an area. For this reason I now prefer to shoot at weekends in preference to Mondays/Fridays, as I am sure that I get better bags of pigeons when there are other shooters in the neighbourhood keeping the birds on the move.

A lofted decoy in position.

A pigeon turning into the wind for landing. The hide can be seen on the right of the photograph.

As regards the organisation of such a shoot, each feeding ground in an area would have to be manned by a gun, and in winter this would, in some districts, require fewer guns than would be needed to cover all the woodlands. In this respect, much depends on what the pigeons are feeding on at the time of the shoot. In snowy weather one can expect the pigeons to be feeding on greenstuffs such as cabbage, brussels-sprouts, kale and turnips—which still remain partly exposed above the snow, if it is not too deep. This type of weather narrows down the number of available feeding grounds considerably, and this is perhaps the best time to hold a shoot of this nature.

January and February are really *the* months of the year to hold these shoots, when food supplies are at a minimum and the pigeons are concentrated on the few feeding grounds available. I am quite confident, however, that this type of shoot, providing that it was properly organised, would give good results in any month of the year. As regards the frequency of these shoots, once a fortnight would probably give the best results, but there again much depends on the number of pigeons in an area, the feeding grounds being used and, in winter, the weather. A sudden spell of severe weather, with plenty of frost and snow, will change the pigeons' diet overnight from acorns and clover to the larger-leafed greenstuffs. During these periods, many farmers with valuable crops to protect have a shooter continuously in attendance, and the organisation of a shoot would simply mean adding guns to the existing staff already in action. On minor feeding grounds or where guns are not available, the use of "rook-scarers" or "bangers" would keep the pigeons on the move.

Summing up, organised shoots, in whichever form they may take, can be an effective means of reducing the number of pigeons in a given area. To be successful, these shoots need careful organisation, straight shooting and shooters who are devoted to the cause. If everyone taking part in these shoots could average one pigeon shot for every two cartridges fired, there would indeed be some goodly bags of pigeons; but at present one dead pigeon for five/ten shots would probably be the average over an area. There is always room for improvement at these shoots, but I am afraid that whilst there are always a few high-spirited individuals attending such occasions, much better results cannot be expected.

9

CALLING, STALKING AND DRIVING PIGEONS

IN the three previous chapters of this book I have covered
the main methods usually adopted for shooting good bags
of pigeons. There are, however, other methods which,
though not producing such large results, nevertheless
assist the general policy of killing pigeons at every oppor-
tunity and thus protecting valuable crops.

In the late spring and summer months when I need one
or two brace of wood-pigeons—perhaps for use as decoys
—I often call the birds within shooting range. Wood-
pigeons begin to "coo" in March and continue throughout
the breeding season until early October. The best period
for calling them, however, is between May and September.

I taught myself to "coo" like a wood-pigeon in my early
shooting days, for it is really not too difficult once one gets
the knack. The basic notes of the call (see page 17) are
the same for all wood-pigeons, but one does hear con-
siderable variations in the tone of the calls of different
birds. Some calls are harsh and throaty; some are sharp
and abrupt; whilst still others sound smooth and alluring.
I always try to imitate the smoother version, and I usually
get a good response (perhaps I sound like a love-sick
male!). The best way to learn the call is by listening to
the call of a wood-pigeon and then to try to imitate it.
With a little practice one should get quite proficient.

The best time of day for calling wood-pigeons is early
morning—soon after dawn. I can visualise one spot where
I could invariably manage to obtain a few birds. I had a
hide built within range of a dead oak tree, which was

situated in a hedgerow leading away from a small fir wood. At day-break on some fine May morning I would wend my way through the dewy grass to my position. First one bird would begin cooing, then another would answer, and soon several birds would be cooing and flapping about inside the wood. A call or two from me would usually attract at least one bird to the edge of the trees, where it would recommence cooing. Another call would bring this pigeon gliding and flapping in its courting-flight towards my tree. The sound of my shot would echo across the small valley, a few more pigeons would hastily depart from the wood, and perhaps another bird would come my way.

Ten minutes or so after the shooting I would call again and another pigeon would answer from somewhere in the wood (no doubt one of the birds that had "sat tight" in the trees during the shooting), and so the process would start again.

Even at a time of day when there are no pigeons calling, if one can set the ball rolling with a good, smooth call then there will often be at least one response from pigeons in the neighbourhood. It is not advisable to answer the call of a pigeon more than three or four times, however, for in my experience if it does not approach during this period it will not come at all. Some pigeons, in fact, are very stubborn and, although they may answer one's calls repeatedly, they will not budge from their tree—presumably they expect the caller to fly to them!

Calling pigeons within shooting range can be extremely useful where there are allotments or gardens whose produce is damaged in the summer months by odd pairs of raiders which have their "base" in an urban area where shooting would be out of the question. One can soon account for several birds during a few early morning visits —much to the gratitude of fellow gardeners.

Altogether, this method of shooting pigeons can be a most efficient way of accounting for numerous birds throughout the breeding season.

Stalking pigeons when they are feeding or resting is another means of shooting them which can on occasions be quite productive. This method is, in fact, complementary to the main methods of shooting pigeons which I have already described in the three preceding chapters. One does not normally set out for a day's stalking, but rather one stalks a flock—or individual birds—as the occasion arises. It quite often happens, for instance, that when one is out decoying, a large flock of pigeons pitches down at the far end of the field in which one is shooting. Here, then, is a time when a stalk is justified—providing pigeons are not still dropping into one's decoys.

Before setting forth on any stalk one must always decide whether or not the pigeons are in a position that will allow one to approach within range of them without being seen. Obviously, a flock sitting 100 yards out from a hedgerow in a flat, open field will not warrant a stalk. But if this same flock were only roughly 40 yards from the hedgerow, a stalk would certainly be in order.

Having decided on a route of approach, I walk as far as I can under cover and then crawl along the ground on my tummy for the remainder of the way. It all really depends on the lie of the land. If there are good open ditches in the area one can often creep along these without any bother. Similarly, thick, low hedges are also ideal for stalking. Remember to keep perfectly still for a minute or so if you disturb a blackbird or some other bird that utters a warning cry. Pigeons are extremely suspicious birds and are soon on the alert if they hear the warning note of another species. I always hold my gun in front of me as I crawl along the ground so that if the pigeons suddenly take flight I am in a position to have a quick shot at them if they happen to be within range. When you take a look to see if you are near the pigeons, always raise your head *very, very slowly*, for a quick movement will often put them in flight. Where possible it is best to peep through some stems of grass or other vegetation so that no clear-cut features are seen by the birds.

Having crept within easy range of a flock, it is then a matter of deciding which bird to fire at. This really depends on the state of alertness of the flock. If the birds have got their heads up in the air and seem ready to depart, then it is best to shoot at once at whichever birds are sitting in line or bunched together. If, however, the birds are still busily feeding and unsuspicious, then one can wait until three, four or even more of them are grouped together before firing. When using a double-barrelled or automatic gun I try to fire my first shot at birds sitting, say, at about 40 yards range, thus leaving any closer birds for a second shot as they rise.

To illustrate this point, I was out shooting one day on a large field of brussels-sprouts which had a long depression running up its centre. There were hundreds of pigeons feeding on the field and occasionally a flock would pitch down in this depression without coming near my hide in the hedgerow bordering the field. Consequently any other pigeons approaching the field would immediately detect the flock and drop in to feed with these birds. A stalk seemed to be the order of the day—if only to disturb the feeding birds.

I crept along the hedgerow until I was level with the flock out in the field and then proceeded to crawl on my hands and knees between two rows of sprouts towards the birds. As I neared the top of the depression, I could hear the pigeons pecking and ripping at the leaves of the sprouts and I knew that I was quite close to the flock. Then I saw one bird go walking across between the rows

and only about 25 yards ahead. I edged forward another
3 or 4 yards on my tummy and then had to lie perfectly
still as another small flock of birds pitched down just in
front of me. Very slowly I raised my head, gun at the
ready, and peeped around a tall plant into the depression.
There were pigeons everywhere. Unfortunately, however,
as the birds were sitting singly on the tops of individual
plants, I could only see two of them in line, and these
were not the closest birds. Nevertheless I decided to fire
at them at once for fear of being spotted by other
approaching birds.

At the shot, the whole air seemed to be thick with
pigeons. I hastily fired my second barrel at another bird
in the thick of the departing flock and three more "dows"
fell amongst the sprouts. Five pigeons to two barrels as
I thought, but when I went to pick them up I found six,
for another bird which must have been sitting between
the plants when I fired my first shot, and which I had not
seen, had also succumbed to the pattern. Of course, one
is not always as fortunate as this, but it does go to show
what can be achieved by careful stalking—and a little
luck.

When a flock of pigeons sitting in a tree decides to drop
down on to a field to feed, they usually do so in ones or
twos—or small batches. Hence, it quite often happens
that an odd bird or two remain sitting in a tree whilst the
remainder of the flock are feeding. It is always advisable,
therefore, to ensure that all the birds in a flock are feeding
in a field before one commences a stalk—unless one can
approach out of sight of the flock and of any "scouts"
sitting in a nearby tree. Otherwise the "scouts" will fly off
in alarm, thus warning their companions of danger.

Stalking pigeons that are sitting in trees is a much more
difficult proposition—especially when the trees are leafless. Except in foggy weather, the birds have a much

better field of vision, and in the majority of cases it is well-nigh impossible to approach within range of them without being spotted. With a thick fog and visibility down to about 30–40 yards, it is a fairly easy matter to stalk within range of pigeons sitting in trees. The main thing to remember is that one should walk very slowly and always hold the gun ready for action. Pigeons rarely fly any distance in a thick fog and after a shot one may find that some birds have landed again in other trees in the vicinity.

When the trees are in full leaf one's chances of stalking pigeons are good, but the snag in this case is that of being able to spot one's quarry amongst the foliage of a tree when one has managed to get within range. I have often stood for a few minutes beneath the thickly-leafed branches of some large oak tree trying to pick out a pigeon at the top of the tree. Eventually the pigeon has spotted me first, and has, of course, flown out of the tree on the wrong side to offer a shot. It is, in fact, usually a case of: (*a*) if you can see the pigeon then the pigeon can see you; or (*b*) if you cannot spot the bird, then it will usually see you first and depart in haste.

Nevertheless, stalking pigeons can be an exciting pastime and besides helping to kill pigeons in fair numbers—and disturbing them from feeding on the farmer's crops—it also gives the shooter much valuable experience in fieldcraft, which can be extremely useful in other forms of shooting—especially wildfowling.

Attempting to drive a flock of pigeons over a shooter (or shooters) can be a very chancy business and is a method of shooting pigeons which I only use as a last resort. One can on occasions combine a drive with a stalk, although this is not usually successful unless the waiting shooter is relatively close to the flock when they are put up. For once the birds are shot at by the stalker they tend to climb very quickly in the air and may well pass over the waiting shooter too high for a shot.

The essential point to remember when driving pigeons is that the shooter to whom the birds are to be driven must keep well out of sight of the flock. For if he is spotted by the birds—even at a distance—then they will certainly not fly over him. There is always a great temptation to peep over a hedgerow to see whether the birds are still there, but this must be avoided at all costs. Patience is indeed a virtue when waiting for pigeons to be driven over one's position.

Before setting off to drive a flock of pigeons that are feeding in a field, one must first of all decide the most likely route that the birds will take in relation to the wind and the presence of woods in the neighbourhood. If pigeons sitting in the centre of a large field are driven into the wind, then usually what happens is that they rise into the wind but then curve away across-wind before a hedgerow is reached. If there is a wood or spinney nearby, and which the birds are frequenting, then one may depend on it that in whichever direction the birds are driven they will invariably alter their course once they are well in the air and head for this sanctuary. Hence, wherever possible, it is best for the waiting gun to position himself on the route he expects the pigeons will take to get to a wood. A typical example of this is shown in the diagram on page 106 (Figure 28).

Driving pigeons that are known to be in a wood can also be attempted, but here again luck plays a big part. When possible it is best to drive the birds into a wind in the hope that they will keep reasonably low. One gun is always quite sufficient to drive pigeons, whilst any number of guns can be positioned around a wood to wait for the birds, providing they do not show themselves to the pigeons *en route* to their positions. It is quite a good policy

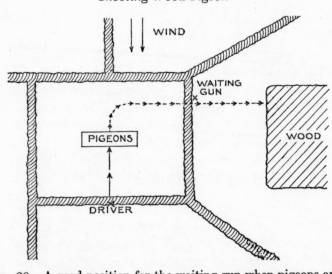

Fig. 28. A good position for the waiting gun when pigeons are
driven into a wind and there is a wood nearby.

to leave one gun along that side of the wood from which
the driver enters, for pigeons often break back over the
driver once in the air.

Compared with the other methods of pigeon-shooting,
driving is probably the least rewarding. Pigeons are such
wary birds that the odds are always on their side, and it
is essential, therefore, for each shooter taking part in a
drive to play his part with calmness and skill. Only in this
way will a good proportion of success be obtained and
many more pigeons accounted for annually.

10

ON OBTAINING PERMISSION TO SHOOT PIGEONS

ALTHOUGH pigeons are a great menace to agricultural crops throughout the country, one cannot simply buy a gun and some ammunition and sally forth on to someone's farm to shoot them. One must always obtain permission from the owner or tenant of a farm before setting foot on his land, and often this can be a difficult task. Farmers, as a whole, are very conservative in their ways, and where game is reared, or a shoot is keepered, there is usually little hope of obtaining a roving commission to shoot pigeons. However, I have found that in all circumstances the personal approach is always the best policy to adopt. It is no use writing to farmers, for, with all due respects, nine times out of ten a reply will not be forthcoming. Whether it is pressure of work or weariness after filling in forms and returns, I do not know, but such is the position.

The way I recommend anyone to set about obtaining permission to shoot pigeons is to first discover by discreet enquiries in the neighbourhood whether anyone already shoots pigeons on the farm that one has in mind. Then, if nobody goes shooting there, wait until pigeons are feeding heavily on a certain field on the farm, then pop along and ask the farmer for permission to shoot pigeons on that field. In many cases the answer will be, "Yes! Certainly!" —and that, at any rate, is a good start. Once a farmer gets to know you, he may offer you a wider scope over his land and even recommend you to a neighbour who is also bothered with pigeons.

Never be afraid to ask a farmer for permission to shoot

pigeons on his land, even though the expected answer is, "No!" One has nothing to lose in any case. Three or four refusals may make one somewhat despondent, but the motto should always be, "Try, try, and try again!" An answer in the affirmative is bound to come if one perseveres, and then one will never look back.

I would seriously recommend any pigeon shooter who also goes wildfowling and rough shooting to join his local Wildfowling Club, if there is one in the district. Most clubs manage to obtain permission for their members to attend organised pigeon shoots on farms and woodlands in the locality, and this at least ensures one of some sport on a few Saturday afternoons of the year.

Once permission to shoot pigeons has been obtained, always try to abide by the following rules:

1. Offer the farmer a brace or two of the bag after a shoot, for even if he may not require them himself, there are always his farm workers to whom he can give them.

2. Never abuse one's privilege in any way. If you have permission to shoot on one field only, then stay there and don't wander about on the other parts of the farm.

3. If you have a pigeon to pick up on another field, always leave your gun (unloaded) in your hide while going to fetch it.

4. If there is game on the farm, never so much as cast a longing eye towards it.

5. Shut any gates behind you and don't climb through and break hedges so that gaps are left through which stock may stray.

6. When shooting pigeons in a wood as they drop in to roost in the late afternoon or evening, always finish shooting in time to allow any pheasants to fly up to roost before it is dark.

7. Never take a friend shooting without first obtaining permission for him to do so.

On obtaining Permission to shoot Pigeons

I find that Ordnance Survey Maps (scale 1 inch to 1 mile or larger) can be very useful when considering the possibility of obtaining some pigeon shooting—especially in a new area. The first things I look for on a map are woodlands, for one may depend that pigeons will frequent them fairly regularly throughout the year. The farmland situated between two woods is certainly worth investigating, for pigeons will be bound to flight between these sanctuaries on some occasions. The contours on a map can also be very helpful when coupled with the knowledge that pigeons will often follow the course of a stream along a valley or pass over the brow of a hill in their travels.

A knowledge of the farm crops that are grown in the district is an advantage, for one can often have a good idea in which direction the pigeons will be flighting at different seasons of the year. After a year or two in the same area, one soon gets to know who grows what, and I often find myself looking forward to sport on a field or meadow long before any pigeons are visiting the spot. Clover, for instance, is a crop that pigeons always favour, especially in late winter and early spring when the young leaves are beginning to show, and some meadows provide good sport every year. Similarly acorns and beech mast attract the pigeons annually in their thousands to our woodlands.

Finally, one must always remember that although farmers are usually very helpful in allowing pigeon shooters on their land, it is a privilege, and as such should be treated with the utmost respect. A little courtesy goes a long way in the sporting world.

★ 11 ★

ON SELLING PIGEONS—AND HOW TO
COOK THEM

WHEN one is shooting pigeons regularly and getting bags of anything from a dozen to fifty or more pigeons the disposal of the birds becomes a problem. The high cost of cartridges makes it essential for the shooter to sell the majority of his bag if he is to meet this expense, and one of the three following methods of selling pigeons is normally used:

(*a*) Selling pigeons to retail shops (e.g. poultry shops and fishmongers).

(*b*) Selling them at a local market or Leadenhall Market in London.

(*c*) Selling them privately to local friends and acquaintances.

Whichever of these three methods is employed there is often little to choose between the prices realised for the pigeons. I consider that if I can get 1*s*. each for my birds, then I am in clover. Usually I am lucky if I get paid 10*d*. each, and quite often when there is a glut of birds, or they are in poor condition, the price is 6*d*. each, or less. Stock-doves or blue rocks are worth about 2*d*. or 3*d*. less than a "woodie".

Let us now consider the three methods of sale in detail. Firstly, selling pigeons to retail shops. One often notices pigeons for sale in the local town in various shops, and the best policy is to approach some of these retailers. Tell them the size of the bags that you normally get, and also the day or days of the week that you go shooting, and they may be able to help you. The only snag with selling to retailers is that usually there is a limited demand for pigeons and one may not be able to dispose of one's bag in this way after every shoot. Nevertheless, one will probably get a slightly better price from a retailer than from the local market, and, after all, every penny counts towards the cost of cartridges.

The second method, selling pigeons at a market, is perhaps the easiest way of disposing of one's birds, but one always has to risk what price they will fetch. Commission, too, is always deducted from the price realised at the auction, and this may be as high as 7½%. A useful guide as to what pigeons are making at the markets can be found in the local newspaper reports for the previous week's auction. Remember that the prices quoted will be before the deduction of commission. In other words, if the report states that pigeons sold at from 1s. to 10d. each, one could expect to get a net price of, say, 10d. to 9d. each. At Leadenhall Market, in London, the various game dealers pay a price that approximates to the price paid by ordinary retail shops, but by the time one has allowed for the cost of carriage in sending the pigeons to London, the net price will probably be considerably less than even local market prices. Personally, I only use markets as a last resort when I cannot sell all my pigeons elsewhere, for only on very rare occasions can one obtain a price equal to or higher than that paid by retailers.

The third method, selling to one's friends and acquaintances, is by far the best way of obtaining a reasonable price for one's birds. Here again, there is a limited demand, but one is always certain of a fair price. I always pick out my best birds for sales of this kind, for there is nothing better to boost one's chances of regular orders than for clients to know that they invariably get fine plump birds with not too much lead in them. I even pluck and draw

111

the pigeons for some of my customers, for it only takes a few minutes once one is used to the job, and it is appreciated. I never charge more than 1s. per bird for private sales, and often I reduce the price according to the condition of the birds. If one charges 50–60% of the price of pigeons for sale in the retail shops, then everyone is satisfied.

Now that we have dealt with the methods of selling pigeons, a few hints on looking after the slain birds prior to disposing of them may prove useful. The period of time that one can safely keep a dead pigeon without it "going-off" depends mostly on the time of the year and temperature of the place of storage. I hang up my pigeons in the garage, which is on the north side of my bungalow and remains reasonably cool except in the summer months. Any odd pieces of string are ideal for this purpose and I tie six or eight pigeons in a bunch. A few nails driven into a wooden rafter at intervals make excellent pegs from which to hang the birds. One does not need anything too elaborate.

In such a place, pigeons will easily keep in good condition for at least a week in cold and frosty weather. When the weather is warmer it is best to dispose of the bag as soon as possible. In fact, when it is really hot weather, pigeons will turn green after only a few hours. During the summer months, therefore, it is hopeless to shoot pigeons for sale unless one has either some refrigeration space available or can take the bag immediately to someone who has. In spring and autumn, given normal temperatures, one can usually keep birds for two or three days prior to selling them, but even so, it is far safer to dispose of them when they are as fresh as possible.

Flies do not become a nuisance until late April, and should never create any real problem. Provided that one is careful to place dead pigeons in a sack or under a piece

Pigeons taking evasive action after a shot. The outstretched wing of a recently shot pigeon can just be seen amongst the decoys on the right of the photograph. One should always ensure that any live-stock are well out of range when shooting. In this case, although the cows appear to be close, they were in fact 200 yards from the hide.

A pigeon retrieved—and more birds approaching? Old clothes are advisable where one has to negotiate barbed-wire fences.

of muslin as soon as they are shot, and keep them covered up continuously from then onwards, no trouble should be experienced. To make doubly certain, a small amount of D.D.T. powder sprinkled over the covering will further deter any flies that are interested. As I have already mentioned in Chapter 6, a sprinkling of D.D.T. over the beak and on the feathers of dead pigeons that are used for decoys will ward off attacks by flies, but it is still advisable to look over the birds for "fly-blows". Inside the beak and nostrils of a dead bird are the two main places that a "blue-bottle" fly chooses to lay its eggs, but it is always wise to look among the feathers generally and especially near any patches of blood. If one finds some eggs, then the only thing to do is to remove them at once and sprinkle some D.D.T. on the infected area of the bird. Remember to keep any bird that has been fly-blown well away from the remainder of the bag so that if some eggs do hatch there is no danger of the maggots crawling on to the other birds. Finally, never sell a pigeon that may inadvertently become fly-blown, for there is always the possibility that a few eggs that one has not removed may hatch out, and it is not good for future sales to supply a customer with a pigeon that quickly "goes off".

As regards preparing a pigeon for the table, I usually pluck the bird, cutting off the wings close to the body in order to simplify matters, for there is not enough meat on them to warrant plucking them. I then remove the crop and cut off the head and neck of the bird close to the breast, and also the feet. The bird can then be drawn as for any other poultry. A thorough wash in cold water completes the operation.

Whenever one happens to be talking to someone about cooking pigeons, the most widely known recipe that springs to mind is, of course, pigeon pie. Of all the famous pies in our cookery I suppose rabbit (prior to myxomatosis),

113

pigeon and rook were the most popular in country districts. If you have not tried pigeon pie, then you do not realise what a delicacy you have been missing. Prepared and cooked in the following way pigeon pie is delicious:

Pigeon Pie

Ingredients: 2 pigeons; ½ lb. rump steak; 2 hard-boiled eggs; a piece of short-crust pastry; 2 slices of bacon; ½ pint of water; salt and pepper.

Method: Prepare the pigeons as described above, and cut each one in half. Cut the steak, bacon and eggs into small slices and place all these ingredients into a pie dish and add salt and pepper. Pour in enough water to half fill the dish and cover the dish with the pastry. Cook on the second shelf of the oven in a medium heat for about 1¼ hours. The pie can then be served either hot or cold.

The second best method to cook a pigeon, in my opinion, is to roast it, and a useful recipe to try is as follows:

Roast Pigeon

Ingredients: 2 pigeons; 2 slices of bacon; 1 onion; 1 packet of stuffing (e.g. sage and onion); breadcrumbs and lard.

Method: Prepare the pigeons as before. Mix the stuffing with a small quantity of breadcrumbs and the onion (chopped up into small pieces) and stuff the birds. Tie a slice of bacon over the breast of each bird. Place the birds in a baking tray with a generous portion of lard and roast in a hot oven for approximately ¾ hour.

My third and last recipe is for pigeon casserole, and a very tasty dish it is!

Pigeon Casserole

Ingredients: 2 pigeons, breasts only; 2 slices of bacon previously fried; ½ lb. stewing steak; 2 potatoes; 2 onions; 2 carrots; 1 lb. mushrooms; flour and seasoning; a small quantity of water or stock and a pinch of mixed herbs.

Method: Pluck the pigeons and cut off the breasts. Place the breasts in a casserole together with the bacon (chopped into small pieces) and the steak (after rolling it in seasoned flour). Add the onions, potatoes, carrots, mushrooms and seasoning. Then half fill the dish with water or stock and add the herbs. Cook in a gentle heat for 2–3 hours.

This recipe is greatly improved by adding a wine glass of dry red wine about halfway through the cooking-time.

★ INDEX ★

117

Index